Elisha Jones

Exercises in Latin Prose Composition

Elisha Jones

Exercises in Latin Prose Composition

ISBN/EAN: 9783337420222

Printed in Europe, USA, Canada, Australia, Japan

Cover: Foto ©Thomas Meinert / pixelio.de

More available books at **www.hansebooks.com**

EXERCISES

IN

LATIN PROSE COMPOSITION:

WITH REFERENCES TO THE GRAMMARS OF

ALLEN AND GREENOUGH, ANDREWS AND STODDARD,
BARTHOLOMEW, BULLIONS AND MORRIS,
GILDERSLEEVE, AND HARKNESS.

BY

ELISHA JONES, A.M.,

ASSOCIATE PROFESSOR OF LATIN IN THE UNIVERSITY OF MICHIGAN;
AUTHOR OF "EXERCISES IN GREEK PROSE COMPOSITION,"
AND OF "FIRST LESSONS IN LATIN."

CHICAGO:
S. C. GRIGGS AND COMPANY.
1888.

PREFACE.

THE aim of this little manual is simply to illustrate such constructions as are most frequently met with in the Commentaries of Caesar, the Orations of Cicero, and similar prose. It does not pretend to teach how to turn all kinds of English into Latin; this could not be expected of so elementary a treatise, and, perhaps, our present systems and methods of preparatory instruction do not demand it: but it designs to give the student such an introduction to the more important principles of Latin syntax, such an acquaintance with the more usual idioms of the language, as shall lead him towards a fuller understanding and appreciation of the great classic prose-writers of ancient Rome. With this end in view, most of the Examples and Vocabularies have been selected from the works mentioned above, and the plan is for the first twenty Lessons to accompany the reading of the Commentaries, and the second twenty the reading of the Orations; though it is hoped that they will not be found out of place in those preparatory schools where other prose is read.

The Exercises are so constructed that, in translation, the style of Caesar and Cicero may be imitated. The treatment of the Moods and Tenses is introduced before that of the Cases, in the belief that the learner should have as extended practice as possible in those difficult subjects. On page 54 a table, based upon a similar table in Roby's Grammar, is given, which is intended to show at a glance the changes necessarily made in the Moods and Tenses when direct Discourse passes into Indirect. In the Notes and Questions an attempt has been made to furnish the beginner all needed assistance through references to the grammar and by means of suggestions rather than by direct information. The principles of syntax referred to and illustrated in each Lesson are, for the most part, reviewed in several of the succeeding Exercises that they may become well fixed in the learner's memory. To make this drill-work still more thorough, there are added, for general review and examination, supplementary Exercises, which are to be recited without previous preparation, and which may enable the teacher to ascertain whether the scholarship of his pupils is well grounded and independent or otherwise. Great pains have been taken to make the General Vocabulary complete; to make it answer questions likely to arise respecting the use of the words employed in the Exercises: deficient Vocabularies are a source of great perplexity and discouragement to beginners. It is believed that these Lessons, if well mastered, will afford sufficient preparation, in the writing of Latin, for admission to any of our American colleges.

The following plan of instruction in Prose Composition, pursued with marked success in many, if not most, of our best preparatory schools, is offered for the benefit of inexperienced teachers. The learner is required to fix in mind the principles of syntax to which the References direct his attention; to commit to memory the Examples and Vocabularies; and to bring to the recitation-room the Exercises carefully translated and written out. These Exercises are copied upon the blackboard, criticised, and corrected when necessary, by both pupils and teacher;

the corrected Exercises are then transferred to a blank book and committed to memory for oral review. The accomplishment of all this will be somewhat difficult when the class is very small and the time short: but the writing upon the blackboard, together with the criticisms and corrections before the whole class, should not be omitted; that which is seen as well as heard is much better remembered than that which only enters the ear.

With many obligations for suggestions from different sources, this book is sent forth in the hope that it may aid somewhat in overcoming the difficulties of Latin syntax, and that its faults may meet with that kindly criticism which has been so generously awarded to its predecessors.

ELISHA JONES.

UNIVERSITY OF MICHIGAN,
    July, 1879.

CONTENTS.

	PAGE.
ABBREVIATIONS.	xii

ARRANGEMENT OF WORDS AND CLAUSES IN LATIN PROSE:
   Usual Order; How to produce Emphasis; Position of Certain Words; Arrangement of Clauses 3

LESSON I.— AGREEMENT:
   Apposition; Predicate Word; Relative Pronouns; Relative Clause made Emphatic 3

LESSON II. — AGREEMENT (*Continued*):
   Finite Verb; Adjectives; Adjectives with Nouns of different Genders; Adjectives as Nouns; Adjectives with the force of Adverbs; Adjectives designating a Certain Part . . . 6

LESSON III. — USE OF PRONOUNS:
   Personal; Possessive; Reflexive 8

LESSON IV. — USE OF PRONOUNS (*Continued*):
   Demonstrative; Indefinite; Relative . . 10

LESSON V. —
   Commands and Exhortations; Prohibitions; Wishes; Vocative 13

LESSON VI. — TENSES OF THE INDICATIVE:
   Historical Present; Present with **dum,** while; Present with **jam, jam diu, jam dudum, jam pridem;** Imperfect; Future; Perfect; Pluperfect; Future Perfect . . . 15

LESSON VII. — SEQUENCE OF TENSES; FINAL CLAUSES:
   Sequence of Tenses; Exceptions; Adverbial Use of Final Clauses; Adjective Use of Final Clauses . . . 18

LESSON VIII. — FINAL CLAUSES (*Continued*):
   Substantive Use of Final Clauses; **ut** omitted . . 21

CONTENTS.

LESSON IX. — CONSECUTIVE CLAUSES:
Adverbial and Adjective Uses of Consecutive Clauses; Substantive Use of Consecutive Clauses 23

LESSON X. — PECULIAR USES OF RELATIVE CLAUSES. — SUBJUNCTIVE WITH QUIN AND QUOMINUS 26

LESSON XI. — CONDITIONAL SENTENCES 28

LESSON XII. — CONDITIONAL SENTENCES (*Continued*):
Supposition contrary to Reality; Use of **quam si, ac si**, etc.; Conditional Relative Clauses; Use of **modo, dum, dum modo** 31

LESSON XIII. — CONCESSIVE CLAUSES 33

LESSON XIV. — CAUSAL CLAUSES. — ATTRACTION . . 36

LESSON XV. — TEMPORAL CLAUSES:
With **postquam, ubi, ut, simulac**; With **antequam, priusquam**; With **cum**; With **dum, donec, quoad** . . 38

LESSON XVI. — DIRECT AND INDIRECT QUESTIONS:
How to Ask a Question; Double Questions; Answers; Indirect Questions; Rhetorical Questions 41

LESSON XVII. — THE INFINITIVE:
Subject of the Infinitive; Infinitive as Subject; Infinitive without Subject-Accusative as Object or Complement . . . 44

LESSON XVIII. — THE INFINITIVE (*Continued*):
Infinitive with Subject-Accusative as Object; Tenses of the Infinitive; Predicate after Infinitive; Historical Infinitive . 47

LESSON XIX. — INDIRECT DISCOURSE . . . 49

LESSON XX. — INDIRECT DISCOURSE (*Continued*): 52
Table showing the Changes made in Moods and Tenses when Direct Discourse becomes Indirect 54

LESSON XXI. — THE GENITIVE:
Subjective Genitive with Nouns; Limited Word omitted; Subjective Genitive with Verbs. 56

LESSON XXII. — THE GENITIVE (*Continued*):
Objective Genitive; Constructions used instead of Objective Genitive; Partitive Genitive; Constructions used instead

of Partitive Genitive; When the Partitive Genitive is not to
be used 59

LESSON XXIII. — THE GENITIVE (*Continued*):
Genitive of Quality; Genitive with Adjectives . . . 62

LESSON XXIV. — THE GENITIVE (*Continued*):
With Verbs of Memory; With Verbs of Emotion; With Verbs
of Judicial Action; With Verbs of Plenty and Want; With
refert and **interest** 64

LESSON XXV. — THE DATIVE CASE:
With Transitive Verbs; Double Construction; With Intransitive Verbs; Dative or Accusative according to Signification;
When "to" and "for" are to be rendered by **ad** and **pro** . 67

LESSON XXVI. — THE DATIVE (*Continued*):
With Compounds; Of the Possessor; Of the Agent; How Intransitive Verbs are used in the Passive 69

LESSON XXVII. — THE DATIVE (*Continued*):
Two Datives; With Adjectives; Other Constructions with
Adjectives; Of Reference 72

LESSON XXVIII. — THE ACCUSATIVE:
Direct Object; With Verbs which in English require a Preposition; With Compounds; Cognate 75

LESSON XXIX. — THE ACCUSATIVE (*Continued*):
Two Accusatives of the same Person or Thing; Two Accusatives — Person and Thing; Two Accusatives with Compound
Verbs; Limit of Motion 77

LESSON XXX. — THE ACCUSATIVE (*Continued*):
Adverbial; Of Specification; In Exclamations; Of Time and
Space 80

LESSON XXXI. — THE ABLATIVE:
Of Separation; Of Source; Of Cause; Of Agent . . 82

LESSON XXXII. — THE ABLATIVE (*Continued*):
Of Manner; Of Accompaniment; Of Means and Instrument;
With certain Deponents; With certain Adjectives . . 85

LESSON XXXIII. — THE ABLATIVE (*Continued*):
With Comparatives; Construction with **plus**, etc.; Measure of
Difference; Ablative of Quality 87

CONTENTS.

LESSON XXXIV. — The Ablative (*Continued*):
Of Price; Of Specification; Of Time; Ablative Absolute . . . 90

LESSON XXXV. — Expressions of Time:
Time When or Within Which; Time How Long or During Which; Use of Prepositions in Expressions of Time; Time Before or After an Event 92

LESSON XXXVI. — Place:
Place From Which; Place To Which; Place At or In Which; Place By, Through, or Over Which; Words used like Names of Towns; Ablative of Place At, In, or On Which; How to express Towards a Place, etc. 95

LESSON XXXVII. — Use of Participles:
Tenses; Different Uses 98

LESSON XXXVIII. — The Gerund and Gerundive . . 101

LESSON XXXIX. — The Gerund and Gerundive (*Continued*) 103

LESSON XL. — The Periphrastic Conjugations. — The Supine 105

EXERCISES FOR GENERAL REVIEW AND EXAMINATION 109

ENGLISH-LATIN VOCABULARY 121

EXERCISES

IN

LATIN PROSE COMPOSITION.

ABBREVIATIONS.

A. & G.	Allen and Greenough's Latin Grammar.
A. & S.	Andrews and Stoddard's Latin Grammar.
B.	Bartholomew's Latin Grammar.
B. & M.	Bullions and Morris's Latin Grammar.
G.	Gildersleeve's Latin Grammar.
H.	Harkness's Latin Grammar, revised edition.
aft.	after.
cf.	**confer,** compare.
decl.	declension.
Ex.	Example.
f.	feminine.
fr.	from.
gram.	grammar.
indecl.	indeclinable.
intr.	intransitive.
lit.	literal, literally.
Ln.	Lesson.
m.	masculine.
n.	neuter.
pl.	plural.
prep.	preposition.
pron.	pronoun.
Ref.	Reference. N. B. A reference, without any mark of punctuation immediately following it, is not to be noticed.
sc.	**scilicet,** understand.
tr.	transitive.
Vy.	Vocabulary.
w.	with.

EXERCISES

IN

LATIN PROSE COMPOSITION.

ARRANGEMENT OF WORDS AND CLAUSES IN LATIN PROSE.

1. *Usual Order.* A. & G. 343, REMARK, *a–d*: A. & S. 279, 1–13 *coarse print*: B. 332 *coarse and fine print*, *d, e;* 333, *a–f*: B. & M. 1385–1398: G. 676, 1–3, REMARK ; 677–684: H. 560 ; 562–568.

2. *How to produce Emphasis.* A. & G. 344, *a–i*: A. & S. 279 7, 9, 16, NOTE 3: B. 332, *a–c*: B. & M. 1386 *Exc.* 2: G. 675, 1: H. 561, I.–III. ; 565 1–3 ; 567 1–3.

3. *Position of Certain Words.* A. & G. 345, *a–d*: A. & S. 279 3 (*c.*), (*d.*), 7 (*b.*), 8, 12: B. 334, *a–d*: B. & M. 1387 1st–5th; 1391 *Exc.* 1 *and* 2: G. 678, REM. 2; 679 REM. 2; 681: H. 569, I.–VI.

4. *Arrangement of Clauses.* A. & G. 345, *e, f*: A. & S. 280, 1–6: B. 335, *a, b*, NOTE: B. & M. 1396–1398: G. 685–687: H. 571; 572, I.–III.; 570.

LESSON I.

AGREEMENT.

REFERENCES.

1, 2. *Apposition.* A. & G. 183; 184, *a*, *b*: A & S. 204, REMARKS 1–5: B. 265, RULE L., REM. 3: B. & M. 622; 626: G. 318; 319: H. 363, 1–3 ; 364.

---

* The numbers of the References correspond with the numbers of the Examples: *e. g.* 1, 2. *Apposition* is illustrated by Examples 1 and 2.

3, 4. *Predicate Word.* A. & G. 185: A. & S. 210, Rem. 1: B. 206, Rule II.: B. & M. 666: G. 324: H. 362, 1.

5-8. *Relative Pronouns.* A. & G. 198; 199; 200, *e*; 201, *a*, *g*: A. & S. 206, (*a.*), (*b.*), (1)-(4), (10), (13) (*a.*), (*b.*): B. 286, *a*, *d*, *i*: B. & M. 683; 693; 694: G. 616, 3, I., II.; 617; 618: H. 445, 1, 3, 4, 7.

9. *Relative Clause made Emphatic.* A. & G. 201 *c*: A. & S. 206 (3): B. 286 *b*, Remark: B. & M. 687: G. 622 ; H. 571, 2.

EXAMPLES.

1. To the town *of Geneva*, **ad oppĭdum** *Genăvam.*
2. We saw Caesar *when boys*, or *when we were boys*, *puĕri* **Caesărem vidĭmus.**
3. Divico was elected *chief*, **Divĭco** *princeps* **creātus est.**
4. Who had come *as ambassadors* to Caesar, **qui** *legāti* **ad Caesărem venĕrant.**
5. With the legion, *which* he had with him, and the soldiers, *who* had assembled, **legiōne,** *quam* **secum habēbat, militibusque,** *qui* **convenērant.**
6. Glory, *which* is the fruit of valor, **gloria,** *qui* **est fructus virtūtis.**
7. Let them be separated from us by a wall, *which* I have often said, **muro,** *id*[1] *quod* **saepe dixi, discernantur a nobis.**
8. Towns and villages, *which* they had burned, **oppĭda vicosque,** *quos* **incendĕrant.**
9. *That part, which* had brought disaster, suffered punishment, *quae pars* **calamitātem intulĕrat,** *ea* **poenas persolvit.**

VOCABULARY I.

across, **trans,** *prep. w. acc.*
always, **semper,** *adv.*
ambassador, envoy, **legātus, i,** *m.*
and, **et, que, ac** or **atque.**[2]
capital, **caput, capĭtis,** *n.*
come, **venio, īre, veni, ventum.**
desire, wish, **volo, velle, volui.**
elect, **creo, āre, āvi, ātum.**
flow into, **influo, ĕre, fluxi, fluxum.**

into, in, on, **in,** *prep. w. acc. aft. verbs of motion ; w. abl. aft. verbs of rest.*
river, **flumen, flumĭnis,** *n.*
see, **video, ēre, vidi, visum.**
send, **mitto, ĕre, misi, missum.**
soldier, **miles, milĭtis,** *m.*
through, **per,** *prep. w. acc.*
to, towards, **ad,** *prep. w. acc.*
with, **cum,** *prep. w. abl.*

EXERCISE I.

1. Caesar[3] sent soldiers into the city of Rome.[3] 2. Soldiers came into the city of Rome to[4] Quintus Metellus, the praetor. 3. Caesar when he was a boy came to Quintus Metellus, the praetor. 4. Caesar and Cicero were elected consuls. 5. Metellus had come as an ambassador to Caesar. 6. The Gauls came as ambassadors through the cities of Rome and Lavinium. 7. The Moselle is a river which flows into[5] the Rhine. 8. Metellus, whom we saw when boys, will be elected consul. 9. Cicero was elected consul, which[6] he had always desired. 10. Caesar will send across the Rhine the soldiers who have come as ambassadors. 11. Caesar sent that legion, which[7] he had with him, across the river Rhine. 12. Metellus sent those soldiers, whom he had with him, into the city of Rome. 13. He sent soldiers into the city of Rome, which[8] is the capital of Italy.

Notes and Questions.

[1] **id** is an *appositive* with the clause **muro discernantur a nobis** and *antecedent* of **quod**.

[2] What difference in the use of **et, que, ac** or **atque**? See A. & G. 156, *a*: A. & S. 198 II. 1 REMARK (*a*.), (*b*.): B. 330 *a*: G. 477–479: H. 554 2, 3.

[3] Words not given in the special vocabularies may be found in the General Vocabulary. In rendering the Exercises into Latin, imitate carefully the Examples.

[4] *To* following a verb of motion and preceding the name of a person must be rendered by the preposition **ad**.

[5] *Into;* although **influere** may have a direct object, Caesar repeats the preposition **in**.

[6] *Which;* what is its antecedent?

[7] Make the relative clause emphatic by placing it first and the antecedent noun in it: see Example 9.

[8] *Which;* see Example 6.

LESSON II.

AGREEMENT (*continued*).

REFERENCES.

1-3. *Finite Verb.* A. & G. 205, *a–d*: A. & S. 209 (*b.*), REM. 12, (2), (5), (7): B. 287 RULE LV. *a*, *b*: B. & M. 634; 643; 644; 646: G. 281, EXCEPTION 1; 283, REM. 1, 2: H. 463, I., II., 1-4.

4, 5. *Adjective.* A. & G. 186, *a–d*: A. & S. 205, REM. 2: B. 265, RULE LI.: B. & M. 650-652: G. 285-288: H. 438, 1; 439.

6-8. *Adjective with Nouns of Different Genders.* A. & G. 187, *b*: A. & S. 205 REM. 2 (1)–(3), EXC. TO REM. 2: B. 268 Rule LII., *a*, *c*: B. & M. 653; 654: G. 282: H. 439 1-3.

9. *Adjectives as Nouns.* A. & G. 188, *b*, *c*: A. & S. 205 REM. 7, (1), (2): B. 269, *a*, *b*: B. & M. 658: G. 195 REM. 1-4: H. 441, 1-2.

10-12. *Adjectives with the force of Adverbs.* A. & G. 191: A. & S. 205 REM. 15: B. 270 *b*; 271: B. & M. 663: G. 324 REM. 6: H. 443.

13. *Adjectives designating a Certain Part.* A. & G. 193: A. & S. 205 REM. 17: B. 274: B. & M. 662: G. 287 REMARK: H. 440 NOTES 1, 2.

EXAMPLES.

1. You and I *did* this, **haec ego et tu** *fecĭmus*.

2. Neither agriculture nor the practice of war *is interrupted*, **neque agricultūra nec usus belli** *intermittĭtur*.

3. A daughter and one of the sons *were taken*, **filia atque unus e filiis** *captus est*.[1]

4. *Genuine* friendships are *everlasting*, **verae**[1] **amicitiae sunt** *sempiternae*.[2]

5. It is *perilous* to cross, **transīre** *periculōsum* **est**.

6. *All* lands and seas, *omnes* **agri et maria**, *or* **agri et maria omnia**.

7. Father and mother are *dead*, **pater et mater** *mortui* **sunt**.

8. Labor and pleasure are *very*[3] *unlike*, **labor voluptasque** *dissimillĭma*.

9. The brave, **fortes**; the fair, **pulchrae**; into winter-quarters, **in hiberna**.

10. Caesar was the first to send, *or* Caesar was the first who sent, **Caesar primus⁴ mīsit.**

11. They came *unwillingly*, *or* they were unwilling to come, *invītī* **venērunt.**

12. They assembled *in very great numbers, frequentissĭmī* **convenērunt.**

13. On the top of the hill, **in summo colle**; into the middle of the city, **in mediam urbem.**

VOCABULARY 2.

alone, **solus, a um.**
cross, **transeo, īre, ii, ĭtum.**
form, draw up, **instruo, ĕre, struxi, structum.**
frequent, **frequens,** *gen.* **frequentis**; see Ex. 12.
glad, **laetus, a, um.**
last, last part of, **extrēmus, a, um.**
meantime, in the meantime, **intĕrim,** *adv.*

middle, middle of, **medius, a, um.**
neither ... nor, **neque ... neque; nec ... nec.**
out of, **ex,** *prep. w. abl.*
top of, **summus, a, um.**
unwilling, **invītus, a, um.**
winter-quarters, **hiberna, ōrum** *n. pl.; properly an adj. w.* **castra** *understood.*

EXERCISE 2.

1. You⁵ and Metellus came unwillingly. 2. Caesar and I⁵ were glad to come. 3. Neither the consul nor the praetor will lead (his⁶) soldiers across the Moselle. 4. The consul and the praetor sent¹² soldiers into the city of Rome. 5. This boy and girl are attentive and industrious. 6. It is perilous for the Germans⁸ to cross the river Rhine and come into France. 7. The brave and the fair come in very³ great numbers to America.⁹ 8. Caesar was frequently in Gaul. 9. The Sequani came alone into the middle of the city. 10. Caesar will be unwilling to send the envoy into the middle of the city. 11. The consul led his soldiers out of camp in the last part of winter.¹⁰ 12. Caesar was the first to lead Roman¹¹ soldiers across the river Rhine. 13. On the top of a hill the consul formed a triple line of the legions, which he had enlisted in Gaul.

Notes and Questions.

[1] **Captus est** agrees with **unus** and is understood with **filia**.

[2] Which is an attributive and which a predicate adjective?

[3] *Very unlike;* the positive with *very* is often rendered into Latin by the superlative; **valde** (*very*) **dissimilia** would be more emphatic.

[4] The adverb, **primum**, would imply that Caesar *first* performed the act of sending and afterwards some other act.

[5] In Latin the first person stands before the second; the second before the third: e. g. **ego et tu; tu et Caesar.**

[6] Words enclosed in parentheses are to be omitted in translation.

[7] *Sent;* See Example 3 and Note 1.

[8] *For the Germans;* render by the Accusative.

[9] *To America;* translate with **in** and the Accusative.

[10] *In the last part of winter;* Is a preposition necessary in the Latin equivalent? What use of the Ablative?

[11] The adjective, **Romānus**, should always follow its noun.

[12] See REF. 1–3.

LESSON III.

USE OF PRONOUNS.

REFERENCES.

1, 2. *Personal.* A. & G. 194, *a, b*: A. & S. 209 REM. 1 (*a.*), (*b.*); 212 REM. 2 NOTE 2: B. 279: B. & M. 1013; 1016: G. 198; 362 REMARK: II. 446, NOTES 1–3.

3–7. *Possessive.* A. & G. 197, *a, c, d, e*: A. & S. 207 REM. 36 (*a.*), (*c.*): B. 173, *a*, REM. 1, 2: B. & M. 1027: G. 299: II. 447; 363, 4, 1).

8–12. *Reflexive (Reflective).* A. & G. 196, *a, f*: A. & S. 208 (*a.*), (*b.*), (1), (5), (6), (*c.*): B. 280 RULE LIV., REM. 1, 2: B. & M. 1018–1020; 1024: G. 294; 295: II. 448, NOTE; 449, 1, 4.

EXAMPLES.

1. *I* am consul, *ego* **sum consul.**
2. Who *of us?* **Quis** *nostrum?*
3. Caesar led out *his* troops, **Caesar copias** *suas* **eduxit.**
4. Gaul is *my* province, **provincia** *mea* **est Gallia.**

5. Ariovistus led *his* troops across the Rhone, **Ariovistus copias trans Rhodănum duxit.**
6. The Gauls made an attack on *our men,* **Galli in nostros impĕtum fecērunt.**
7. Their own province, **sua** *ipsōrum* **provincia.**
8. They surrendered *themselves* and *their possessions* to Caesar, *se su*a**que Caesări dedidērunt.**
9. The king demanded that Caesar send an envoy to *him,* **rex postulāvit ut Caesar legātum ad** *se* **mittĕret.**
10. Our soldiers having encouraged *one another,* **nostri cohortāti** *inter se.*
11. All differ *from one another,* **omnes** *inter se* **diffĕrunt.**
12. They give hostages *to one another,* **obsĭdes** *inter sese* **dant.**

VOCABULARY 3.

amusing, **delectans, antis.**
attack, **impĕtus, us,** *m.*
betake one's self, **se conferre; confĕro, conferre, contŭli, collātum.**
bring on, **infero, inferre, intŭli, illātum.**
chief, leading, **princeps, ĭpis,** *adj.*
encourage, **cohortor, āri, ātus sum.**
entrust, **commendo, āre, āvi, ātum.**
fire, set fire to, burn, **incendo, ĕre, cendi, censum.**

from, out of, **e, ex;** from, from near, **a, ab;** *prepositions w. abl.*
lead out, **edūco, ĕre, duxi, ductum.**
march, **iter, itinĕris,** *n.*; to march, **iter facĕre; facio, facĕre, feci, factum.**
on, upon, in; see *Vy.* 1 *under* into.
parts, from all parts, **undĭque,** *adv.*
state, **civĭtas, ātis,** *f.*
surrender, **dedo, ĕre, dedĭdi, dedĭtum.**
vigorously, **acrĭter,** *adv.*

EXERCISE 3.

1. You are that consul who was the first[1] to lead Roman soldiers across the river Moselle. 2. Who of you[2] has sent envoys to the king? 3. We shall lead out our troops from camp and make an attack on the enemy. 4. The Gauls have betaken themselves into their own[3] province. 5. The enemy will betake themselves to their (friends) and make

an attack on our (men). 6. I shall surrender myself and all my (possessions) to Caesar. 7. The king demanded that we send[4] you to him as an envoy. 8. The soldiers are very unwilling to go through the middle of their own city. 9. In the last part of your book is a very amusing story. 10. All these nations gave hostages to one another. 11. Our soldiers are crossing the Rhine, which[5] is very perilous. 12. We shall march into the towns and villages which the enemy have set fire to. 13. The enemy came in very great numbers and occupied the top of the mountain. 14. The chief (men) will assemble from all parts and entrust themselves and their states to Caesar. 15. Our (soldiers), having encouraged one another, made a vigorous attack[6] on the Gauls.

Notes and Questions.

[1] *first;* what would **qui primum duxisti** imply? See Ln. II., Note 4.

[2] *of you;* which form of the Genitive plural of personal pronouns is used partitively? See A. & G. 99 *b:* A. & S. 212 Rem. 2 Note 2: B. 227 Note: B. & M. 773 *last part:* G. 99 Rem. 1: H. 446 Note 3.

[3] *own;* See Example 7.

[4] *that we send;* See Example 9.

[5] *which;* what is its antecedent and gender? See Ln. I., Ref. 5-8, and Ex. 7.

[6] *made a vigorous attack;* translate as if it read, *made an attack vigorously.*

LESSON IV.

USE OF PRONOUNS (*Continued*).

1-8. Demonstrative. A. & G. 195, *e*, *f:* A. & S. 207 Rem. 20, 23, 25, 27, 28: B. 281-285: B. & M. 1028; 1029; 1032; 1034; 1035; 1039: G. 290-293; 296-298: H. 450, 1, 2; 451, 3; 452, 1, 2.

9-13. Indefinite. A. & G. 202, a-c; 203, a-c: A. & S. 207

LATIN PROSE COMPOSITION. 11

Rem. 30-33: B. 173 *e*, 1, 3, 6, *f:* B. & M. 1047-1049: G. 300-306: H. 455-458; 459.

14, 15. Relative. A. & G. 201 *e*, *g:* A. & S. 206 (17): B. 286 *h:* B. & M. 701: H. 453.

EXAMPLES.

1. They hastened to *that* place, **ad eum locum contendērunt.**
2. They send envoys to *him*, **legātos ad** *eum* **mittunt.**
3. Caesar grasps *his* right hand, **Caesar** *ejus* **dextram prendit.**
4. They perform *the same* (act), *idem* **faciunt.**
5. You *also*, or *likewise*, said, **vos** *iīdem* **dixistis.**
6. Caesar *himself* hastened to them, **Caesar** *ipse* **ad eos contendit.**
7. *You* surrendered yourself, *tu* **te** *ipse* **dedidisti.**
8. They were fighting on the *very* banks, **in** *ipsis* **ripis proeliabantur.**
9. Without *any* danger, **sine** *ullo* **pericŭlo.**
10. He asked that Caesar send *some one*, **rogāvit ut Caesar alĭquem mittĕret.**
11. If *any* wars should occur, **sī** *qua* **bella incidĕrint.**
12. One man from one ship, another from another, **alius alia ex nave.**
13. They were carried, some in one direction, some in another, **alii aliam in partem ferebantur.**
14. When *these* had betaken themselves into the town, *qui* **cum se in oppĭdum contulĕrant.**
15. They killed a multitude as great *as* was the length of the day, **tantam multitudĭnem interfecērunt,** *quantum* **fuit diēi spatium.**

VOCABULARY 4.

any, any one, anybody, anything, **alĭquis**; *aft.* **si, nisi, ne,** *or* **num, quis**; *see gram. for declension.*
as much ... as, as great ... as, **tantus, a, um ... quantus, a, um.**
as soon as, **simul atque.**[1]
at once, **statim,** *adv.*
direction, **pars, partis,** *f.*
grasp, **prehendo (prendo), ĕre, prehendi, prehensum.**
hasten, **contendo, ĕre, tendi, tentum.**
party, the one party ... the other, **altĕri ... altĕri.**
reach, **capio, capĕre, cepi, captum.**
rescue, **eripio, eripĕre, eripui, ereptum.**
right hand, **dextra, ae,** *f., sc.* **manus.**

save, **servo, āre, āvi, ātum.**
singularly, **egregie,** *adv.*
some, somebody, some one, something, **alĭquis; quidam;** *see gram. for decl.*

some ... others, **alii ... alii.**
time, at one and the same time, **simul,** *adv.*
withdraw, **se recipĕre; recipio, recipĕre, recēpi, receptum.**

EXERCISE 4.

1. These went[2] unwillingly, but those were very glad to go.[2] 2. By means of[3] these (men) he will rescue himself and save his country. 3. We shall hasten to them ourselves and likewise demand hostages. 4. They betook themselves to Metellus, governor of Africa, and also[4] son-in-law of a king. 5. We also[4] sent envoys to him[5] and betook ourselves into a town singularly fortified by nature. 6. We can not cross this river without some danger. 7. We grasped their right hands and Marcus did the same. 8. We shall send soldiers into their very[6] cities, if they carry on[7] any war with us.[8] 9. Our army occupied as much of their city as it was able to occupy. 10. Some of the Gauls, as soon as they reached the top of the hill, began at once to fortify their[9] camp. 11. Some betook themselves into cities, others into forests and swamps. 12. The one party will withdraw upon a mountain, the other will betake themselves to their baggage and carts. 13. One man came from one city, another from another. 14. At one and the same time, the shouts of those who were coming with the horses were heard, and we were sent, some in one direction and some in another.

Notes and Questions.

[1] Also written **simulatque, simul ac,** and **simulac.**
[2] Write the verb but once, and at the end of the entire sentence.
[3] *By means of;* **per** with Accusative.
[4] *Also;* see Ex. 5.   [5] *to;* see LN. I, NOTE 4.
[6] *Very;* when used to emphasize a noun, *very* should be rendered by the proper form of **ipso:** see Ex. 8.

7. *Carry on;* render by the future.

8. *With us;* what is the position of **cum** when used with a personal or relative pronoun? See A. & G. 99 *c;* 104 *e;* A. & S. 133 REM. 4: B. 334 *d;* B. & M. 986: G. 414 REM. 1: H. 184 6; 187 2.

9. *Their;* how should it be rendered? See LN. III., REF. 8-12.

LESSON V.

COMMANDS AND EXHORTATIONS: PROHIBITIONS: WISHES: VOCATIVE.

REFERENCES.

1, 2. *Use of the Imperative.* A. & G. 269: A. & S. 267, REM. 1: B. 312 RULE LXXI.: B. & M. 1110: G. 259-261; 263: H. 487.

3, 4. *Subjunctive in Commands and Exhortations.* A. & G. 266: A. & S. 260 REM. 6: B. 309, *b, d*, RULE LXVIII.: B. & M. 1197; 1198: G. 256, 1-3: H. 483, 3; 484, II., IV.

5-7. *How to express a Prohibition.* A. & G. 269 *a;* A. & S. 267 REM. 3: B. 309 *c;* 313 REMARK: B. & M. 1113; 1114: G. 264 II.; 266: H. 488; 489, 1)-3).

8, 9. *How to express a Wish.* A. & G. 267, *b;* A. & S. 260 REM. 6, (*a*), (*b*); 263: B. 309 *a*, RULE LXVIII.: B. & M. 1193-1196: G. 253; 254: H. 483, 2; 484, I.

1. *Use of the Vocative.* A. & G. 241, *a;* A. & S. 240: B. 210 RULE VI.: B. & M. 974: G. 194 REM. 3: H. 369.

EXAMPLES.

1. Leap down, soldiers, **desilīte, milītes.**

2. Lead out your (associates); purify the city, **educ tuos; purga urbem.**

3. Let us not go, **ne eāmus.**

4. Let them either go out or keep quiet, **aut exeant aut quiescant.**

5. Do not hesitate, **noli dubitāre, nolīte dubitāre.**

6. Do not do this, you shall not do this, **hoc ne fecĕris.**

7. Do not pardon, **cave ignoscas.**

8. Would that he had led out his forces! **utĭnam copias suas eduxisset!**

9. O that I were not living! **utĭnam ne vivĕrem!**

10. May my fellow-citizens be prosperous! **sint florentes cives mei!**

VOCABULARY 5.

advance, **progredior progrĕdi, progressus sum.**
assemble, **convenio, ire, vēni, ventum.**
as soon as possible, **quam primum,** *adv.*
begin a battle, **proelium committo, ĕre, mīsi, missum.**
break up camp, **castra moveo, ĕre, mōvi, mōtum.**
face about, wheel about, **signa converto, ĕre, verti, versum.**
flee, **fugio, fugĕre, fugi, fugĭtum; terga verto, ĕre, verti, versum.**

happy, **beātus, a, um.**
hesitate, **dubĭto, āre, āvi, ātum.**
lead out, **edūco, ĕre, duxi, ductum.**
prosperous, **florens,** *gen.* **florentis,** *adj.*
put to flight, **in fugam do, dăre dĕdi, dătum.**
right, **dexter, dextra, dextrum**
take, capture, **capio, capĕre, cepi, captum.**
wing, **cornu, us** *n.*; on the right wing, **a dextro cornu.**

EXERCISE 5.

1. Lead out all your troops as soon as possible, general,[1] and take the enemy's camp. 2. Soldiers, break up camp as soon as possible and advance into the enemy's country. 3. Wheel about; attack the English; put them to flight. 4. Let us likewise face about as soon as possible and make an attack on the French. 5. Let us not[2] assemble in very great numbers,[3] but let us flee, some in one direction and some in another. 6. Let the boys and girls be both attentive and industrious. 7. Do not hesitate, soldiers, to march through the very territory of the Gauls. 8. Do not begin the battle on the right wing, but withdraw at once upon this mountain. 9. You shall[4] not march through our territory. 10. May you and all your friends

be happy and prosperous![5] 11. Would that our soldiers had not fled! would that they were advancing into the very territory of the enemy![5] 12. O that our men had broken up camp! O that they were beginning battle on the left wing! 13. Let us not surrender ourselves and all our possessions[6] to Caesar. 14. Do not surrender yourselves and all your possessions to Metellus, the consul. 15. O that some of the Gauls would surrender themselves and all their possessions to me![5]

Notes and Questions.

[1] In Latin prose the Vocative usually stands after one or more words of its sentence.

[2] *Not;* in negative sentences expressing an exhortation or a wish, ne is generally used; see Examples 3 and 9.

[3] *Very great numbers;* see LN. II., REF. 10–12 and NOTE 3.

[4] *Shall not march;* see Ex. 6.

[5] What kind of a wish is expressed by this sentence?

[6] *Possessions;* is it necessary to translate this word?

LESSON VI.

TENSES OF THE INDICATIVE.

REFERENCES.

1. *Historical Present.* A. & G. 276 *d:* A. & S. 259 (1) (*a.*): B. 58: B. & M. 1082: G. 220: H. 467 III.

2. *Present with* dum, *while.* A. & G. 276 *c:* A. & S. 259 (1) (*c.*): G. 220 REMARK: H. 467 4.

3. *Present with* jam, jam diu, jam dudum, jam pridem. A. & G. 276 *a:* A. & S. 145 1. 2: B. 58: B. & M. 1083: G. 221: H. 467 2.

4–6. *Imperfect.* A. & G. 277, *a*, *c:* A. & S. 145 II., 1: B. 59: B. & M. 1087–1089: G. 222–224: H. 469 I., II.

7. Future. A. & G. 278, b: A. & S. 145 III.: B. 56 a: B. & M. 1090: G. 234, Rem. 1: H. 470, 1.
8, 9. Perfect. A. & G. 279, a, Remark: A. & S. 145 IV., Remark: B. 60: B. & M. 1092; 1093; 1095: G. 226–228, Rem. 1; 231; 232: H. 471, I., II., 1, 3.
10. Pluperfect. A. & G. 280: A. & S. 145 V.: B. 56 b: B. & M. 1096: G. 233, Rem. 1: H. 472.
11. Future Perfect. A. & G. 281, Remark: A. & S. 145 VI.: B. 56 b: B. & M. 1098: G. 236, Rem. 2, 3: H. 473, 2.

EXAMPLES.

1. *They send* envoys to Caesar with respect to a surrender, **legātos ad Caesărem de deditiōne** *mittunt*.
2. While *he was delaying*, fear seized the army, **dum** *morātur*, **timor exercĭtum occupāvit**.
3. *We have been living* now a long time in the midst of these perils, **jam diu in his perícŭlis** *versāmur*.
4. The shouting of those, who *were coming, was arising*, **eōrum, qui veniēbant, clamor oriebātur**.
5. *They kept making* sallies from the town, **ex oppĭdo excursiōnes** *faciēbant*.
6. *They were wont to talk* (*used to talk*) more fearlessly than they fought, **fortius** *loquebantur* **quam pugnābant**.
7. If *they are willing* to hasten, *they will overtake* (him), **si accelerāre** *volent, consequentur*.
8. The enemy *fled*, **hostes** *terga vertērunt*.
9. He remembers all, **omnia memĭnit**; men hated him, **eum odĕrant viri**.
10. Who *had come* as envoys to Caesar, **qui legāti ad Caesărem** *venĕrant*.
11. When you are reading this, perhaps *I shall have met* him, **cum tu haec leges, ego illum fortasse** *convenĕro*.

VOCABULARY 6.

because, **quod**, *conj.*
commend, **laudo, āre, āvi, ātum**.
delay, **moror, āri, ātus sum**.
devastate, **vasto, āre, āvi, ātum**.
for the sake of, **causā**: *abl. of cause; must follow its limiting gen.*
sally, **excursio, ōnis,** *f.*
scatter, rout, **fugo, āre, āvi, ātum**.
supplies, **commeātus, us,** *m.*

surrender, **deditio, ōnis,** *f.*
take part, **versor, āri, ātus sum.**
time, now a long time, for a long time, **jam diu, jam dudum.**
to-day, **hodie,** *adv.*
vicinity, in the vicinity of, **ad,** *prep. w. acc.*

when, **cum (quum),** *conj.*
while, **dum,** *conj.*
winter, pass the winter, **hiĕmo, āre, āvi, ātum.**
with respect to, **de,** *prep. w. abl.*

EXERCISE 6.

1. The king pitches a camp and sends envoys to the consul with respect to a surrender. 2. While the general was forming[1] a triple line of battle on the top of the hill, the enemy made an attack on him. 3. The governor has been delaying[2] now a long time in the vicinity of this city for the sake of[3] supplies. 4. The Gauls were devastating the territory through which they had come. 5. The Germans used to cross the river Rhine with[4] rafts and boats. 6. The French kept making sallies from the town and attacks on the Germans. 7. The enemy had now for a long time been making[5] sallies from the town of Geneva. 8. If our men make[6] a sally from the town to-day, they will take the enemy's camp. 9. We likewise were wont to make sallies from the city and take part with our friends in battles. 10. Caesar marched through the territory of the Gauls, who at once surrendered themselves and all their possessions to him.[8] 11. Caesar remembered all that he had ever[7] seen. 12. While our general was delaying in those places for the sake of supplies, ambassadors from a large part of Gaul came to him[8] with respect to peace. 13. He commended the legions, which were wintering in the neighborhood of Geneva, because they had been the first to march into the enemy's country. 14. When you and I lead[9] our troops across the river Rhine, we shall scatter the Germans, some in one direction and some in another.

Notes and Questions.

¹ *was forming;* see REF. 2 and EX. 2.
² *has been delaying;* see REF. 3 and EX. 3.
³ *for the sake of;* what must be the position of **causa?** see VY.
⁴ *with rafts;* should a preposition be used in the Latin equivalent?
⁵ *had been making;* with **jam diu,** ETC., the Latin employs the imperfect where the English uses the progressive pluperfect.
⁶ *make;* what tense must be used? See REF. 7 and its EX.
⁷ *ever,* in the sense of *at any time,* must be rendered by **umquam**; in the sense of *always,* by **semper.**
⁸ *to him;* how should *to him* be rendered in Sentence 10 and how in Sentence 12? Why?
⁹ *lead;* with what tense should *lead* be rendered and why? See REF. 11.

LESSON VII.

SEQUENCE OF TENSES. — FINAL CLAUSES.

REFERENCES.

1-7. *Sequence of Tenses.* A. & G. 283-286: A. & S. 259, A, B, I., 1, 2: B. 61; 311 Rule LXX.: B. & M. 1163, I., II.; 1164: G. 216; 510: H. 490; 491; 492, 1, 2; 493, 1, 2.

8, 9. *Exceptions.* A. & G. 287, *a, c:* A. & S. 258 REM. 1, 2: B. 311 *g.* REM. 2: B. & M. 1167; 1171: G. 511 REM. 1, 2: H. 495, I.-IV.

10, 11. *Adverbial use of Final Clauses.*¹ A. & G. 317, *b:* A. & S. 262, REM. 5, 9: B. 298, *a,* 1, REMARK, 2; RULE LXI.: B. & M. 1205; 1207, (*a.*); 1210: G. 543; 544, I.; 545, 1-3: H. 497, II., 1, 2.

12, 13. *Adjective use of Final Clauses.* A. & G. 317: A. & S. 264 5: B. 299: B. & M. 1207, (*b.*); 1212: G. 632: H. 497, I.

EXAMPLES.

1. He stays	that he may know,	remănet	
2. He will stay	to know, in order	remanēbit	ut sciat.
3. He has staid	to know, so as	remansit	
4. He will have staid	to know.	remansĕrit	

5. He was staying that he might know, **remanēbat**
6. He staid to know, in order **remansit** } **ut sciret.**
7. He had staid to know, so as to know; **remansĕrat**
8. I have been waiting that you might see, **exspectāvi ut vidērētis.**
9. He persuades Dumnorix to attempt the same, **Dumnorĭgi, ut idem conarētur, persuādet.**
10. He strengthens the forts *that he may be able* more easily to prevent, **castella commūnit,** *quo* **facilius prohibēre** *possit.*
11. He stopped *that he might not lose* time (*so as not to lose* time), **constĭtit** *ne* **tempus** *dimittĕret.*
12. He sends forward scouts *to select* (*who are to select*) a place, **exploratōres praemittit** *qui* **locum** *delĭgant.*
13. He sent forward the cavalry *to delay* (*which was to delay*) the army, **equitātum,** *qui* **agmen** *morarētur,* **praemīsit.**

VOCABULARY 7.

auxiliaries, **auxilia, ōrum,** *n. pl.*
avoid, **vito, āre, āvi, ātum.**
bridge, **pons, pontis,** *m.*
cavalry, **equitātus, us,** *m.*
confer, **collŏquor, i, locūtus sum.**
cut down, **interscindo, ĕre, scĭdi, scissum.**
easily, **facĭle,** *adv.*
excuse, **excūso, āre, āvi, ātum.**

fear, **timor, ōris,** *m.*
force, band, body, **manus, us,** *f.*
fort, **castellum, i,** *n.*
infantry, **pedĭtes, um,** *m. pl.*
nation, **natio, ōnis,** *f.*
send forward, **praemitto, ĕre, mīsi, missum.**
storm, **expugno, āre, āvi, ātum.**
suspicion, **suspicio, ōnis,** *f.*
terrify, **perterreo, ēre, ui, ĭtum.**

EXERCISE 7.

1. Crassus and Metellus go into Italy that they may be elected[1] consuls. 2. The cavalry delay in the vicinity of the enemy's camp so as to avoid[1] the suspicion of fear. 3. The infantry had delayed in the vicinity of the city in order to avoid the suspicion of fear. 4. The consul was leading a large force of cavalry[2] through the territory of the Allobroges, that he might terrify them. 5. Metellus sent forward his cavalry, which was to terrify the Gauls.

6. These had delayed, that they might avoid the suspicion of fear. 7. We have been storming the city that the enemy might not[3] make a sally from it.[4] 8. Ariovistus sends forward his infantry with all his cavalry, which forces are to terrify our men. 9. The Gauls sent ambassadors to me when I was consul, who were to confer with me[5] with respect to peace. 10. The consul led with him[6] a large force of infantry that he might more easily storm the fort. 11. Let the general send forward a part of his[8] infantry to storm the fort and cut down the bridge. 12. Let us march into the enemy's country that he may not winter in ours. 13. Crassus will march into Aquitania and Helvetia that auxiliaries may not be sent from those nations into Gaul. 14. While the general was delaying[9] in the vicinity of Geneva for the sake of[10] supplies, men from a large part of Helvetia came to him to excuse[1] themselves.

Notes and Questions.

[1] In English, *purpose* or *design* is expressed by *that* and a verb with *may* or *might;* by *in order, so as, who is, who was,* ETC. followed by an *infinitive;* and very often by an *infinitive* alone: see Examples.

[2] *Large force of cavalry;* when a Noun is modified both by an Adjective and a Genitive, the usual order is Adj., Gen., Noun; e.g., **tanta rerum commutatio.**

[3] *That not* in a *final clause* should be rendered by **ne.**

[4] *It;* what must be the gender of this word in the Latin? Why?

[5] What is the position of **cum** when used with personal and relative pronouns? See LN. IV., NOTE 8.

[6] *Him;* with what pronoun should *him* be rendered? See LN. III., REF. 8–12.

[7] *That;* how may *that* be rendered when it introduces a final clause containing a comparative?

[8] *His;* when should *his, their* be rendered by **suus**? When by the Genitive of **is**?

[9] *was delaying;* see LN. VI., REF. 2.

[10] What must be the position of **causa** with respect to its limiting Genitive? See VY. 6.

LESSON VIII.

FINAL CLAUSES (*Continued*).

REFERENCES.

1-14. *Substantive Use of Final Clauses.* A. & G. 329; 331, *a-f:* A. & S. 273, 1, 2, 4; 262 REM. 7: B. 295, 1, 2, RULE LVIII.: B. & M. 1200: G. 544 II.; 546; 552: H. 498, I.-III.

12-14. **ut omitted.** A. & G. 331 *f.* REMARK: A. & S. 262 REM. 4: B. 295 REMARK: B. & M. 1203; 1204: G. 546 REM. 3: H. 499 2.

EXAMPLES.

1. He advised *that* the legions *unite*, **monuit** *ut* **sese legiōnes** *conjungĕrent.*
2. They ask him *to choose*, **ab eo postŭlant** *uti deligat.*
3. They begged him *not to move*, **ne movēret petiērunt.**
4. He exhorted them *to withstand* the attack, **cohortātus est** *uti*[1] **impĕtum** *sustinērent.*
5. He commanded *that they should not throw back* any weapon, **imperāvit** *ne* **quod telum** *rejicĕrent.*
6. He ordered these *to find out*, **his mandāvit** *ut cognoscĕrent.*
7. They persuade their neighbors *to set out*, **persuādent finitĭmis** *uti proficiscantur.*
8. He employs the Senones *to find out* these things, **dat negotium Senonĭbus** *uti ea cognoscant.*[2]
9. He feared that he would offend, **ne offendĕret verebātur.**
10. I fear that you are not long lived, **ut sis vitālis metuo.**
11. I fear that I shall not bring it to pass, **timeo ne non impetrem.**
12. I desire you to consider, **velim existĭmes.**
13. He asks him to make an end, **rogat finem faciat.**
14. Him he orders to go to the Belgians, **huic mandat Belgas adeat.**

VOCABULARY 8.

advance to the attack, make an assault, **signa infĕro, inferre, intŭli, illātum.**

advise, **moneo, ēre, ui, ĭtum.**
at all, **omnīno,** *adv.*
beg, **peto, ĕre, īvi & ii, ītum.**

command, **impĕro, āre, āvi, ātum,** *w. dat.*
employ, **negotium do, dare, dedi, datum;** *lit.* give employment; *w. dat. of person employed and final clause defining the employment.*
exhort, urge, encourage, **cohortor, āri, ātus sum.**
fear, **vereor, ēri, ĭtus sum; timeo, ēre, ui; metuo, ĕre, metui, metūtum.**
fearlessly, bravely, **fortĭter,** *adv.*
find out, **cognosco, ĕre, cognōvi, cognĭtum.**

persuade, **persuadeo, ēre, suāsi, suāsum.**
report, **refĕro, referre, retŭli, relātum.**
remaining, rest of, **relĭquus, a, um.**
throw back, **rejicio, rejicĕre, rejēci, rejectum.**
unite, join together, **conjungo, ĕre, junxi, junctum,** *w. reflexive pronoun.*
weapon, **telum, i,** *n.*
withstand, **sustineo, ēre, tinui, tentum.**

EXERCISE 8.

1. The consul advised that for the future we avoid all suspicions of fear. 2. The general exhorts both the cavalry and infantry to advance fearlessly to the attack. 3. Crassus advises that the legions unite and make an assault on the enemy. 4. The governor betook himself to his friends[3] and urged them[3] to assemble in as great numbers as possible.[4] 5. Caesar betook himself to his men[3] and commanded them not to throw back any weapon at all. 6. Metellus sent ambassadors to the king, who were to beg[5] him not to cut down the bridge. 7. We shall employ these soldiers to cut down the bridge. 8. They employed us to find out what Ariovistus said[6] and to report to them.[7] 9. They persuaded us to pass the winter in their city. 10. We have persuaded not only the boys but also the girls to be more attentive and industrious. 11. We fear[8] that father and mother will be unwilling to come. 12. Our general feared that auxiliaries would come from those nations into Switzerland. 13. We have feared that you and the rest of the boys would not be attentive. 14. The

general fears that his cavalry will not withstand the attack of the Swiss. 15. Him he desired to go⁹ as an ambassador to the French.

Notes and Questions.

¹ **uti**, original form of **ut**.

² **uti — cognoscant**, an appositive with **negotium**; what is the literal translation of this sentence?

³ Is it necessary to render this word?

⁴ *as possible;* the force of a superlative is intensified by prefixing **quam**: e.g. **quam plurimi**, *as many (men) as possible*.

⁵ *who were to beg;* which use of the Final Clause? See L<small>N</small>. VII., R<small>EF</small>. 12, 13.

⁶ *said;* render by the Imperfect Subjunctive.

⁷ *them;* what pronoun should be used? See L<small>N</small>. III., R<small>EF</small>. 8-12.

⁸ Verbs and expressions of *fearing* in Latin are followed by **ne** and the Subjunctive if the object is not desired; by **ut** or **ne non** and the Subjunctive if it is desired. In such sentences **ne** equals *that, lest;* **ut, ne non** equal *that not:* see Examples 9, 10, 11.

⁹ *to go;* see Example 12.

LESSON IX.

CONSECUTIVE CLAUSES.

REFERENCES.

1-3. *Adverbial and Adjective Uses of Consecutive Clauses.*¹ A. & G. 319, R<small>EM</small>., *a*, R<small>EM</small>.: A. & S. 262, R<small>EM</small>. 1, 5 *fine print;* 264 1: B, 300, 1, 2; 301, 1, 2, Rule LXII.: B. & M. 1218-1220: G. 553-556; 633: H. 500, I., II.

4-8. *Substantive Use of Consecutive Clauses.* A. & G. 332, *a, b, e, f:* A. & S. 262 R<small>EM</small>. 3; 273 1 (*b.*): B. 296, R<small>ULE</small> LIX., R<small>EMARK</small>; 297, *d:* B & M. 1222-1224: G. 557-559: H. 501, I., 1, 2, II., 1, 2, III.; 502, 1, 2.

EXAMPLES.

1. Such a change was made *that* our soldiers *renewed* the battle, **tanta commutatio facta est,** *ut* **nostri proelium** *redintegrārent.*

2. There are so many *that* a prison *can not* hold them, **sunt ita multi,** *ut* **eos carcer capĕre** *non possit.*

3. No one will be so stupid *as not to see,* or *that he will not see,* **nemo tam stultus erit,** *qui non videat.*

4. It happened *to be* full moon, **accĭdit** *ut esset* **luna plena.**

5. The result was *that they endured* not even one attack, **factum est,** *ut* **ne unum quidem impĕtum** *ferrent.*

6. They made the departure *seem* entirely like a flight, **fecērunt,** *ut* **consimĭlis fugae profectio** *viderētur.*

7. They had caused these hedges *to furnish* protection, **effecĕrant,** *ut* **hae sepes munimenta** *praebērent.*

8. It is a law of war *that they* who conquer rule, **jus est belli** *ut,* **qui vicĕrint,** *impĕrent.*[2]

VOCABULARY 9.

arise, **coorior, ĭri, ortus sum.**
bring to pass, cause, **efficio, efficĕre, effēci, effectum.**
defend, **defendo, ĕre, fendi, fensum.**
endure, bear, **fero, ferre, tuli, latum.**
happens, the result is, it comes to pass, **fit, fiĕri, factum est.**
indeed, at least, **quidem,** *adv.; stands immediately after the emphatic word.*
nobody, no one, **nemo;** *gen. and abl. supplied from* **nullus;** *dat. and acc.,* **nemĭni, nemĭnem.**
not ... even, **ne ... quidem;** *the word to be made emphatic must stand between* **ne** *and* **quidem.**
remains, it remains, **relĭquum est; restat.**
seize, **occŭpo, āre, āvi, ātum.**
so, **tam, ita,** *adv's.*
spiritedly, **acrĭter,** *adv.*
storm, **tempestas, ātis,** *f.*
such, so great, **tantus, a, um;**
such, of such a kind, **talis, e.**
suddenly, **subĭto,** *adv.*
true, **verus, a, um.**
wicked, **imprŏbus, a, um.**

EXERCISE 9.

1. Such fear suddenly seized the army that it terrified the minds of all. 2. Such a storm suddenly arose that it drove our ships, some in one direction and some in another. 3. Our soldiers are so cowardly that they will not[3] advance[4] to the attack. 4. No one is so cowardly as not to defend himself. 5. The consul made us betake

ourselves into the middle of the city. 6. We fear that we shall not make you hear. 7. I brought it to pass that the senate sent me as an ambassador* to the French. 8. The result was that the Gauls did not endure even one attack of our men but[5] fled at once. 9. It happens that the very[6] men, who are making an assault on the Swiss, are very[7] cowardly. 10. It remains for you to go[8] to the general and beg him not to pitch his camp in our city. 11. It is a law of war that those, who have been conquered, surrender[9] themselves and all their possessions. 12. The storm was so great that nobody[3] came. 13. The consul advised that no one[3] lead his army out of winter-quarters. 14. For a long time I have been exhorting[10] the cavalry to make a spirited assault on the English. 15. This is indeed true that he exhorted[11] us to withstand the attack.

Notes and Questions.

[1] In English a *result* is expressed by *that*, *so that*, and an *indicative*; by *as*, *so as*, and an *infinitive*; sometimes by an *infinitive* alone. The preceding clause generally contains some word modified by *such* or *so*: see Examples and compare LESSON VII., NOTE 1.

[2] **ut — impĕrent** is an appositive with **jus**.

[3] *that not*; In clauses of result, *that not*, *that no one*, *that nothing*, *that never* are to be translated respectively by **ut non, ut nemo, ut nihil, ut numquam**; in clauses of purpose by **ne, ne quis, ne quid, ne umquam**.

[4] *will advance*; "The present subjunctive corresponds in most cases to the present and to the simple future of the indicative; but when it is important to distinguish the future from the present, the future active participle, with **sim** or **essem**, is resorted to." Roby, 1507.

[5] *but*; "If a negative proposition is followed by an affirmative, in which the same thought is expressed or continued, **que, et,** or **ac**, is employed in Latin, where in English we use *but*." Madvig, 433 Obs. 2.

[6] *very*; see LN. IV., NOTE 6.   [7] *very*; see LN. II., NOTE 3.

[8] *for you to go*; translate as if it read, *that you go*.

[9] *that — surrender*; see Ex. 8 and NOTE 2.

[10] *have been exhorting*; see LN. VI., REF. 3.

[11] *that he exhorted*; which use of the Consecutive Clause?

LESSON X.

PECULIAR USES OF RELATIVE CLAUSES. — SUBJUNCTIVE WITH QUIN AND QUOMINUS.

REFERENCES.

1-9. *Relative Clauses.* A. & G. 320, *a, b, f:* A. & S. 264 6, 7, 9, 10, : B. 301, 3, 4, 5, Remark : B. & M. 1226; 1227: G. 633; 634: H. 503, I., II., 1-3.

10-12. *Subjunctive with Quin.* A. & G. 319 *d:* A. & S. 262 Rem. 10: B. 297, Rule LX., Remark: B. & M. 1230-1233 : G. 550; 551, 1, 2: H. 504, 1-3, 1), 2), 4.

13, 14. *Subjunctive with Quominus.*[1] A. & G. 319 *c:* A. & S. 262 Rem. 9, *last part:* B. 297, Rule LX., Remark : B. & M. 1236: G. 547; 549: H. 497 2.

EXAMPLES.

1. And not any one has been found *who refused* to die, **neque repertus est quisquam,** *qui mori recusāret.*

2. There was nothing *with which to allay* hunger, **nihil erat,** *quo* **famem** *tolerārent.*

3. There is nobody *who does* not *fear* you, **nemo est** *qui* **te non** *metuat.*

4. There are some *who do* not *see,* **sunt** *qui* **non** *videant.*

5. There will be some *who will desire,* **erunt** *qui velint.*

6. What is there *which can* please you ? **Quid est** *quod* **te delectāre** *possit ?*

7. I am *the only man who could* not be induced, *unus* **ego sum** *qui* **addūci non** *potuĕrim.*

8. He will not be a fit man to send, **non erit idoneus qui mittātur.**

9. The stories are not worth reading, **fabŭlae non dignae sunt quae legantur.**

10. I do not doubt *that he will inflict* punishment, **non dubĭto** *quin* **supplicium** *sumat.*

11. There is no doubt that they are the most powerful, **non est dubium quin plurĭmum possint.**

12. They could not be restrained *from hurling* weapons, **retinēri non potĕrant** *quin* **tela** *conjicĕrent.*

13. Nobody was hindered *from enjoying* his property, **nemo impediebātur** quomĭnus[1] **ejus rebus** fruerētur.

14. They will not refuse *to be* under their government, **non recusābunt** quomĭnus[1] **sub illōrum imperio** sint.

VOCABULARY 10.

allay, endure, **tolĕro, āre, āvi, ātum.**
doubt, **dubĭto, āre, āvi, ātum.**
doubtful, **dubius, a, um**; there is no doubt that, **non est dubium quin,** *w. subj.*
dwell in, inhabit, **incŏlo, ĕre, colui,** *no sup.*
fit, suitable, proper, **idoneus, a, um.**
government, **imperium, i,** *n.*
hinder, **impedio, īre, īvi or ii, ītum.**
hostage, **obses, obsĭdis,** *m. and f.*
hunger, **fames, is,** *f.*

induce, **addūco, ĕre, duxi, ductum.**
inflict punishment, **supplicium sumo, ĕre, sumpsi, sumptum;** to inflict punishment on any one, **de alĭquo supplicium sumĕre.**
prevent, **deterreo, ēre, ui, ĭtum.**
refuse, **recūso, āre, āvi, ātum.**
restrain, **retineo, ēre, tinui, tentum.**
severe, **gravis, e.**
time, a second time, **itĕrum,** *adv.*
under, **sub,** *prep. w. acc. and abl.*
worthy, **dignus, a, um.**

EXERCISE 10.

1. A storm arose which drove[2] our ships, some in one direction and some in another. 2. We have nothing with which to allay our hunger. 3. There was nobody who did not fear that[3] you would come. 4. There are some who fear that[3] our infantry will not be able to withstand the attack. 5. Who is there in this city that will not bravely defend[4] himself? 6. Diviciacus was the only man who could not be induced to give his children as hostages. 7. This is the only general who urged his soldiers to march[5] fearlessly into the enemy's country. 8. This man is not fit to be sent as ambassador to the Germans. 9. The books, which you sent me,[6] are worth reading a second time. 10. We did not doubt that Ariovistus would inflict

very severe punishment on all the hostages. 11. There is no doubt that he will inflict severe punishment on all of us.⁷ 12. We shall not be able to prevent even the Germans⁸ from uniting themselves with the French. 13. Our army could not be restrained from making an attack on the Swiss. 14. The Romans were not hindered from marching through the territory of the Gauls. 15. The Germans do not refuse to be under our government, but are glad to dwell in our country.

Notes and Questions.

¹ Some write **quominus**; others **quo minus**. "The use of '**quominus**' springs from the euphemistic courtesy of the Latin language. It is more polite to say, 'I will hinder you so that you shall *the less* do what you wish,' than to say, '**quin (ut non) facias**,' 'so that you shall *not* do it.' So after **recuso** the refusal is less point blank, as far as expression goes, with '**quominus**' than it would be with **quin**." Moberly's Caesar, page 225, Note P. 18.

² *which drove;* the indicative would simply state the fact that 'the storm drove our ships'; the subjunctive, that 'it was of such force as to drive them': which mood should be used?

³ *that;* see Ln. VIII., Note 8.

⁴ *will defend;* see Ln. IX., Note 4, *last part.*

⁵ *to march;* see Ln. VIII., Ref. 1-14.   ⁶ *me* = to me = **ad me**.

⁷ *all of us* = *us all.*

⁸ *Germans;* what must be the position of **Germānos**? Why? See Vy. IX., under *not — even.*

LESSON XI.

CONDITIONAL SENTENCES.

REFERENCES.

1-15. A. & G. 304, *a*, Note, *b, d;* 306; 307, *a–d:* A. & S. 261, 2, Rem. 1, 2: B. 305, *a*, 1, 2, *b;* 306, Note, *a*, Remark, *b*, Rule LXVI.: B. & M. 1259-1266: G. 590-592; 596-598: H. 506; 507, I., II.; 508, 1-5; 509, Note 1.

EXAMPLES.

1. If they are fighting, they are conquering, — **si pugnant, vincunt.**
2. If they were fighting, they were conquering, — **si pugnābant, vincēbant.**
3. If they have fought, they have conquered,
   If they fought, they conquered, — **si pugnavērunt, vicērunt.**
4. If they fight (shall fight), they will conquer, — **si pugnābunt, vincent.**
5. If they fight (shall have fought), they will conquer, — **si pugnavĕrint, vincent.**
6. If they shall have fought, they will have conquered, — **si pugnavĕrint, vicĕrint.**
7. If they should fight, *or* were to fight, they would conquer.
   If they should be fighting, they would be conquering, — **si pugnent, vincant.**
8. If they should have fought, they would have conquered,
   If they should fight, they would conquer, — **si pugnavĕrint, vicĕrint.**

9. If he has come, he has brought a legion with him, **si venit, secum legiōnem duxit.**
10. I shall not make war upon them, if they pay (shall pay) the tax, **iis non bellum inferam, si stipendium pendent.**
11. If he leaves (shall have left), I shall reward him, **si discessĕrit, illum remunerabor.**
12. If nobody should follow, I should go with the tenth legion, **si nemo sequātur, cum decĭma legiōne eam.**
13. Unless relief is dispatched (shall be dispatched), I cannot hold out, **nisi subsidium summittētur, ego sustinēre non possum.**
14. Leap down unless you wish to abandon the standard, **desilīte, nisi vultis aquĭlam prodĕre.**
15. But if you prefer that, betake yourself to Caesar, **sin id mavis, confer te ad Caesărem.**

VOCABULARY II.

alarm, **commoveo, ēre, mōvi, mōtum.**
depart, **discēdo, ēre, cessi, cessum.**
flight, **fuga, ae,** *f.*
give, **do, dare, dedi, datum.**
if, **si**; if however, but if, **sin,** *conj's.*
make upon, bring upon, **infĕro, inferre, intŭli, illātum;** *w. acc. and dat.*
pay, **pendo, ĕre, pependi, pensum.**
prefer, **malo, malle, malui.**
stay, **remaneo, ēre, mansi,** *no sup.*
tax, **stipendium, i,** *n.*
tenth, **decĭmus, a, um.**
unless, **nisi.**
write, **scribo, ēre, scripsi, scriptum.**

EXERCISE II.

1. If these boys and girls are attentive and industrious, they are happy. 2. If the flight of the Gauls has alarmed any, they have fled. 3. If the Romans were marching through Gaul, the Gauls were making war upon them. 4. If any of the soldiers were cowardly, the general inflicted severe punishment upon them. 5. If nobody comes, we shall go with the tenth legion alone. 6. They would not make war upon us, if we should pay the tax. 7. If hostages should be given, I should make peace with them. 8. If there should be no doubt that hostages would be given, I should be willing to make peace with them. 9. If they should not refuse to be under our government, nothing would prevent us from making peace with them. 10. Do not break up camp, unless you wish to begin a battle. 11. But if you prefer to break up camp, betake yourselves to the vicinity of Geneva. 12. If you were to wheel about, you would put the enemy to flight. 13. If you wrote these books yourself, they are worth reading. 14. If there is nobody in this city who will bravely defend himself, let us flee. 15. Stay in this place, if you wish to avoid the suspicion of fear.

LESSON XII.

CONDITIONAL SENTENCES (*Continued*).

1 - 5. *Supposition contrary to Reality.* A. & G. 308: A. & S. 261, 1 : B. 306 c, RULE, LXVI., *last part:* B. & M. 1267 ; 1268: G. 599: H. 507, III.; 510, NOTE 1.

6. *Use of* **quam si, ac si,** *etc.* A. & G. 312, REMARK: A. & S. 263, 2: G. 604: H. 513, II.

7. *Conditional Relative Clauses.* A. & G. 316: B. 307 RE-MARK: B. & M. 1280: G. 594: H. 507 2.

8. *Use of* **modo, dum, dum modo.** A. & G. 314: A. & S. 263 2 *last part*, NOTE: B. & M. 1259 *last part;* G. 575: H. 513, I.

EXAMPLES.

1. If they were fighting, they would be conquering, **si pugnārent, vincĕrent.**
2. If they had fought, they would have conquered, **si pugnavissent, vicissent.**
3. If they could, they would storm the fort, **si possent, castellum expugnārent.**
4. If they had been able, they would have cut down the bridge, **si potuissent, pontem interscidissent.**
5. If the troops had come, we should be storming the fort, **si copiae venissent, castellum expugnarēmus.**
6. They shudder at the cruelty of the absent Ariovistus as if he were present (i.e., as they would shudder if he were present), **absentis Ariovisti crudelitātem, velut si adsit, horrent.**
7. Whoever sees this will be compelled to admit that there are gods, *or,* if any one should see this, he would be compelled to admit that there are gods, **haec qui videat, cogātur confitēri deos esse.**
8. Let him depart, provided he goes into exile, **discēdat, dum modo in exsilium eat.**

VOCABULARY 12.

absent, **absens,** *gen.* **absentis.**
affair, **res, rei,** *f.*
arrival, **adventus, us,** *m.*

as if, **velut si, quasi.**
beset closely, **urgeo, ēre, ursi,** *no sup.*

by, **a, ab,** *prep. w. abl.*
cruelty, **crudelĭtas, ātis,** *f.*
district, **regio, ōnis,** *f.*
inform anyone, **alĭquem certiōrem facio, facĕre, feci, factum**; be informed, **certior fio, fĭĕri, factus sum.**
in person, **coram,** *adv.*
lead down, **dedūco, ĕre, duxi, ductum.**
on the march, **ex itinĕre**; to be on the march, **esse in itinĕre.**

present, be present, **adsum, adesse, adfui.**
provided, **modo, dum, dum modo,** *conj's.*
regard as an enemy, **pro hostĕ habeo, ēre, ui, ĭtum.**
seventh, **septĭmus, a um.**
shudder at, **horreo, ēre, horrui,** *no sup.*
well, **bene,** *adv.*

EXERCISE 12.

1. If the infantry could cross the river, they would storm the fort on the march. 2. If the Gauls had cut down the bridge, they would not have been able to cross the river. 3. If he had not led down his army out of these districts, I should have regarded him as an enemy. 4. If he were leading down his army out of these districts, we should not regard him as an enemy. 5. Unless he leads[1] down his army out of these districts, I shall regard him as an enemy. 6. But if he should lead down his army out of these districts, we should not regard him as an enemy. 7. The Sequani used to shudder[2] at the cruelty of the absent Ariovistus as if[3] he were present in person. 8. The king makes us shudder at[4] his cruelty as if he were present in person. 9. If any one[5] should be alarmed by the flight[6] of the Gauls, he would flee. 10. If the enemy had been informed with respect to our arrival, they would have fled. 11. If we should employ the Gauls to inform[7] us with respect to his[8] arrival, it would be well. 12. If Caesar had employed the Gauls to inform him with respect to these affairs, it would have been well. 13. If the general saw[9] that the legions were closely beset[10] by the ene-

my, he would advise that they join themselves together. 14. If Caesar had seen that the seventh legion was closely beset, he would have advised that the legions unite and attack the enemy. 15. Nothing will prevent us from visiting[11] you, provided we are not sick.

Notes and Questions.

[1] *leads;* what tense should be used?
[2] *used to shudder at;* see LN. VI., REF. 4–6.
[3] *as if;* what may be supplied between *as* and *if?*
[4] *shudder at;* see LN. IX., REF. 4–8, and EX. 6.
[5] *If anyone;* see REF. 7 and EX. 7.
[6] *by the flight;* what does this phrase denote? should a preposition be used in the Latin equivalent?
[7] *to inform;* what must be its construction? See LN. VIII., REF. 1–14, and EX. 8.
[8] *his;* how is it to be translated?
[9] *saw;* what time does this verb refer to, present or past? What tense must be used?
[10] *that the legions were closely beset,* **legiōnes urgēri.**
[11] *from visiting;* see LN. X., REF. 13, 14.

LESSON XIII.

CONCESSIVE CLAUSES.

REFERENCES.

1–6. *Use of Moods in Concessive Clauses.* A. & G. 313, *a–f;* 326; A. & S. 263 2 (1), (4), 5 REMARK 1 (*a*) *last part:* B. 292 *e,* RULE LVI.; 303, RULE LIV.: B & M. 1281–1284; 1290: G. 605–610; 637; 588: H. 514; 515, I., II., 1–3, III.

EXAMPLES.

1. I opposed you although I saw my own ruin, **tibi obstĭti, quamquam vidēbam perniciem meam.**

2. Although all perils threaten, I shall endure them, **licet perīcŭla impendeant omnia, subībo.**

3. Although the Suevi had not been able to drive these out, yet they made them tributary to themselves, **hos cum Suevi expellĕre non potuissent, tamen vectigāles sibi fecērunt.**

4. Although the battle was fought till evening, nobody could see an enemy in retreat, **cum ad vespĕrum pugnātum sit, aversum hostem vidēre nemo potuit.**

5. However large it is, it is too little, **quamvis amplum sit, id est parum.**

6. Even if the zeal of men should fail, the gods would compel, **etiam si homĭnum studia deficiant, dii cogant.**

VOCABULARY 13.

although, **quamquam, cum (quum), licet,**[1] *conj's.*

drive out, **expello, ĕre, pŭli, pulsum.**

fight, **pugno, āre, āvi, ātum**; *in passive used impersonally;* **pugnātur,** it is fought, a battle is fought, they fight.

harbor, **portus, us,** *m.*

however, however much, **quamvis,** *conj.*

nevertheless, yet, still, **tamen,** *adv.*

now, **jam, nunc,** *adv's.*

nothing, **nihil,** *indecl. neut. substantive.*

offend, **offendo, ĕre, fendi, fensum.**

plan, **consilium, i,** *n.*

reprimand, **accūso, āre, āvi, ātum,**

rout, put to flight, **fugo, āre, āvi, ātum.**

safely, **tuto,** *adv.*

sail, **navĭgo, āre, āvi, ātum.**

scout, **explorātor, ōris,** *m.*

severely, **gravĭter,** *adv.*

teacher, **praeceptor, ōris,** *m.*

till late at night, **ad multam noctem.**

tributary, **vectigālis, e,** *adj.*

EXERCISE 13.

1. Although the Gauls are leading down their troops out of these districts, nevertheless we shall regard them as enemies. 2. Although our men fought bravely till late at night, still they were not able to storm the fort. 3. Although these boys and girls are now attentive and industrious, yet their teacher will severely reprimand them. 4. Although they cannot drive out the Aquitani from their territory,[2] nevertheless they will make them tributary

to themselves.³ 5. Although the legions were closely beset, the seventh suddenly wheeled about and put the enemy to flight. 6. Although our troops kept making sallies from the town till late at night, still they did not rout the English. 7. Although Caesar sent forward scouts, who were to inform⁴ him with respect to the plans of the Gauls, nevertheless they made no report.⁵ 8. Although he feared that⁶ he would offend the mind of Diviatiacus, he urged his soldiers to withstand the attack bravely. 9. However much you desire to see us, we shall not visit you. 10. Even if the governor sends⁷ men to cut down the bridge, the enemy will cross the river and storm the town. 11. Even if the general should employ scouts to inform him with respect to the plans of the enemy, they would make no report. 12. Even if Caesar had been informed with respect to the plans of the Gauls, he would have urged the Romans to send an army into their⁸ country.

Notes and Questions.

¹ licet is properly an impersonal verb, present tense; hence it is followed only by the *Present* and *Perfect* Subjunctive; cf. rule for Sequence of Tenses, LN. VII., REF. 1-7.

² *from territory;* abl. without preposition.

³ *themselves;* what pronoun should be used? See LN. III., REF. 8-12.

⁴ *who were to inform;* see LN. VII., REF. 12, 13.

⁵ *they made no report* = *they reported nothing.*

⁶ *that;* how should "that" be rendered after a verb of fearing? "that not"?

⁷ *sends;* what time does this verb refer to? What mood and tense should be used in translating it? See LN. XI., Examples 4 and 5.

⁸ *their;* render with the genitive plural of **ille** because it refers to Gauls, the remoter word.

LESSON XIV.

CAUSAL CLAUSES. — ATTRACTION.

REFERENCES.

1-5. *Causal Clauses.* A. & G. 321, *b;* 326; 341, *d:* A. & S. 263 5, Rem. 1 (*a.*); 264 8; 266 3: B. 292, *c;* 302, 1-3, Rule LXIII.: B. & M. 1250; 1251; 1255: G. 538-542; 587: H. 516, I., II.; 517.

6. *Attraction.* A. & G. 342; *also read the* Note *immediately preceding* 340: A. & S. 266: B. 310, Rule LXIX.: B. & M. 1291: G. 666: H. 529, II.

EXAMPLES.

1. Our men were thrown into great disorder, because they could not keep in line, **nostri, quod non ordines servāre potěrant, magnopěre perturbabantur.**

2. Since he makes this requital, I demand this, **quoniam hanc gratiam refert, haec postŭlo.**

3. He complains because he has been forsaken, **quod sit destitūtus,**[1] **querītur.**

4. Caesar is doing a great wrong, *because he is making* the revenues decrease, **magnam Caesar injuriam facit,** *qui* **vectigalia deteriōra** *faciat.*

5. Since he had come unexpectedly, the Remi sent envoys, **cum de improvīso venisset, Remi legātos misērunt.**

6. Such an opinion of the war was spread abroad, that envoys were sent by those tribes which *dwelt* across the Rhine, **tanta belli opinio perlāta est, uti ab iis nationĭbus, quae trans Rhenum** *incolěrent,*[2] **mitterentur legāti.**

VOCABULARY 14.

because, **quod, quia,** *conj's.*
beyond, across, **trans,** *prep. w. acc.*
bring on, **infěro, inferre, intŭli, illātum.**
complain, **queror, queri, questus sum.**

follow, follow close after, **subsěquor, sěqui, secūtus sum.**
get a firm footing, **firmĭter insisto, ěre, instĭti,** *no sup.*
greatly, **magnopěre,** *adv.*
hitherto, **adhuc,** *adv.*

keep in line, **ordĭnes servo, āre, āvi, ātum**; *lit.* keep ranks.
lately, **nuper,** *adv.*
ravage, **popŭlor, āri, ātus sum.**
renew, **redintegro, āre, āvi, ātum.**
run, **curro, ĕre, cucurri, cursum.**
severely, **gravĭter,** *adv.*

since, **cum (quum), quoniam,** *conj's.*
spread abroad, **perfĕro, perferre, pertŭli, perlātum.**
support, **sublĕvo, āre, āvi, ātum.**
the one party . . . the other, **altĕri . . . altĕri.**
throw into disorder, **perturbo, āre, āvi, ātum.**

EXERCISE 14.

1. Our soldiers will be thrown into great[3] disorder, because they can neither keep in line nor follow the standards. 2. Your men were thrown into disorder, because one was running from one ship, another from another. 3. The infantry were thrown into great disorder, because they could neither get a firm footing nor follow the standards. 4. Caesar did a great wrong, because he inflicted[4] so severe punishment on the Gauls. 5. The consul censures his soldiers severely, because he is not supported by them. 6. Caesar complains because the Britons have brought on[5] a war without cause. 7. Since they could no longer[6] withstand the attacks of our men, the one party betook themselves into the town, the other to their baggage and wagons. 8. The Aedui complain because the Germans, who have lately come into Gaul, are ravaging their territory. 9. Such an opinion of this war will be spread abroad, that envoys will be sent to us by the nations which dwell beyond the Alps. 10. Such a change was made that the soldiers, who had hitherto been cowardly, renewed the battle. 11. He complains because he has been hindered from renewing[7] the battle. 12. There is no doubt that he will inflict[8] severe punishment on the infantry, because they did not advance to the attack. 13. There were some who complained,[9] because the cavalry kept making sallies from the town.

Notes and Questions.

¹ **quod sit destitūtus**; the writer does not vouch for the reality of this reason but states it as that given by him who complains and hence uses the subjunctive; had he written **est** instead of **sit**, then he would have stated it as the *actual reason* according to his own view.

² **quae incolĕrent**; "Subordinate sentences are often found with the verb in the Subjunctive, because they are stated not as a fact but as part of a thought. The principal sentence which they qualify has its verb in the infinitive or subjunctive." Roby, 1772. Such a construction is called "*Subjunctive by Attraction.*"

³ *great;* see Ex. 1.

⁴ *because he inflicted;* A Causal Clause, introduced by a relative pronoun, has its verb in the subjunctive.

⁵ *because . . . have brought on;* In translating a Causal Clause, which is to begin with **quod**, think whether the writer is stating the actual reason, according to his own view, or a reason given by some other person than himself; in the former case render with the indicative; in the latter, with the subjunctive.

⁶ *no longer* = *not longer.*   ⁷ *from renewing;* see Ln. X., Ref. 13, 14.

⁸ *will inflict;* see Ln. IX, Note 4, and Ln. X., Ref. 10-12.

⁹ *who complained;* see Ln. X., Ref. 1-9 and Ex. 4.

LESSON XV.

TEMPORAL CLAUSES.

REFERENCES

1, 2. *With* **postquam, ubi, ut, simulac.** A. & G. 323; 324: A. & S. 259 Rem. 1 (2) (*d.*): B. 292 *d* 1, Rule LVI.: B. & M. 1249; G. 563; H. 518.

3, 4. *With* **antequam, priusquam.** A. & G. 327, *a:* A. & S. 263 3: B. 292 *d*, 2, Rule LVI.; 304, 2, Rule LXV.: B. & M. 1241; 1243, *Obs.* 2, 3: G. 576-579: H. 520, I., 1, 2, II.

5-7. *With* **cum (quum).** A. & G. 325: A. & S. 263 5, Rem. 2: B. 292 *d* 1, Rule LVI.; 304 1, Rule LXV.: B. & M. 1244; 1245: G. 582; 586: H. 521, I., II., 1, 2.

8-10. *With* **dum, donec, quoad.** A. & G. 328: A. & S. 263 4: B. 292 *d*, 3, Rule LVI.; 304 3, Rule LXV.: B. & M. 1238; 1239: G. 571; 573; 574: H. 519, I., II., 1, 2.

EXAMPLES.

1. *After he saw* the troops, he pitched a camp, *postquam* copias vidit, castra posuit.
2. When he comes, he sets forth the fear, ubi venit, timōrem propōnit.
3. *Before* the enemy *recovered* from fright, he led his army into the territory of the Suessiōnes, *priusquam* se hostes ex terrōre recipĕrent, in fines Suessiōnum exercĭtum duxit.
4. He arrived in the vicinity of the enemy's camp *before* the Germans *could* find it out, *prius* ad hostium castra pervēnit, *quam* Germāni sentīre *possent*.
5. *When* Caesar *was* in Gaul, reports were brought to him, *cum esset* Caesar in Gallia, ad eum rumōres afferebantur.
6. When he had come, he ascertained this, cum venisset, ea cognōvit.
7. He came to the army himself, *as soon as there began* to be a supply of food, ipse, *cum primum* pabŭli copia esse *incēpit*, ad exercĭtum venit.
8. He waited *until* the rest of the ships *assembled*, *dum* relĭquae naves *convenīrent*, exspectāvit.
9. Wait until he is made consul, exspectāte dum consul fiat.
10. While this was taking place, he arrived, dum haec geruntur, pervēnit.

VOCABULARY 15.

after, postquam, *conj.*
arrive, pervenio, īre, vēni, ventum.
as a deserter, pro perfŭga.
as soon as, cum (quum) primum.
away, be away, absum, abesse, abfui or afui.
begin, incipio, cipĕre, cēpi, ceptum.
before, antĕquam, priusquam, *conj's.*
bring to, affĕro, afferre, attŭli, allātum.
far, longe, *adv.*

frequent, creber, crebra, crebrum.
fright, terror, ōris, *m.*
hasten, contendo, ĕre, tendi, tentum.
increase, augeo, ēre, auxi, auctum, *tr.:* cresco, ĕre, crevi, cretum, *intr.*
receive, accipio, cipĕre, cēpi, ceptum.
recover, recipio, cipĕre, cēpi, ceptum, *w. reflexive pron.*
return, revertor, i, versus sum.
set forth, propōno, ĕre, posui, posĭtum.

take place, **geror, i, gestus sum.**   wait, **exspecto, (expecto), āre, āvi, ātum.**
there, in that place, **ibi,** *adv.*
until, till, **dum, donec, quoad,** *conj's.*   when, **ubi, cum (quum),** *conj's.*

EXERCISE 15.

1. When he came to them as a deserter, he set forth the fear of the Roman people. 2. After the lieutenant was informed by those scouts, whom he had sent, that all the forces of the Germans were not far away,[1] he led his army across the Moselle, which is in the territory of the Belgae, and there pitched his camp. 3. Metellus led his army into the country of the Allobroges, before the enemy recovered from fright. 4. Before the enemy recover[2] from fright, our general will lead his cavalry into the territory of the Swiss, who are nearest to the Germans, and hasten towards the town of Geneva. 5. When we were in Italy, frequent reports were brought to us and we were informed by letter[3] that the French had made war upon the Germans. 6. You hastened into Italy yourself as soon as the Germans began to make war upon the French. 7. We shall hasten into Switzerland as soon as the summer begins[4] to be hot. 8. Our general waited until the enemy assembled in very great numbers. 9. Let us not wait until the forces of the enemy are increased[5] and their cavalry returns.[6] 10. When we had arrived in the vicinity of the forest and had begun to fortify a camp, suddenly from[7] all parts of the forest the enemy made an attack on our men. 11. While this was taking place[8] among the Helvetii, Crassus arrived in the territory of the Aquitani with those troops which he had received from[7] Caesar.

Notes and Questions.

[1] *Were away,* **abesse**; what must be the case of its subject?
[2] *recover;* "In reference to future time, these particles (**antequam,**

priusquam) take the present and future perfect indicative; rarely the present subjunctive." A. & G.

3 *by letter;* Ablative of means.
4 *begins;* render with the Future Indicative.
5 *Let us not wait;* see Ln. V., Ref. 3, 4, and Note 2.
6 *are increased . . . returns;* see Ex. 9.
7 *from;* which preposition should be used, **ex** or **ab**?
8 *While this was taking place;* see Ex. 10 and Ln. VI., Ref. 2.

LESSON XVI.

DIRECT AND INDIRECT QUESTIONS.

REFERENCES.

1-5. *How to ask a Question.* A. & G. 210, *a–f*: B. 328, *a,* Rem. 1: B. & M. 1040; 1041; 1103–1106: G. 451–458; 464–467: H. 351, 1, Notes 1–3, 2.

6. *Double Questions.* A. & G. 211, *a–d*: A. & S. 265 Note 2 Rem. 2: B. 328 *b*, Rem. 1: B. & M. 1107; 1108: G. 460; 461; 459: H. 353, 1, 2, Notes 2–4.

7, 8. *Answers.* A. & G. 212: B. 328 *a* Rem. 2, *b* Rem. 2: G. 473: H. 352, Notes 1, 2.

9-14. *Indirect Questions.* A. & G. 334, *a, f, with Note immediately preceding* 334: A. & S. 265, Note 2: B. 294, *a,* Rule LVII.: B. & M. 1182: G. 462, 1–4; 469: H. 528 2 Note; 529, I., 1, Note 1, 3.

15. *Rhetorical Questions.*¹ A. & G. 268: A. & S. 260 Rem. 5: B. 308 *b*, Rule LXVII.: B. & M. 1180: G. 468: H. 486 II.

EXAMPLES.

1. Which states are in arms? **quae civitātes in armis sunt?**
2. Do you remember? **meministīne?**
3. Is not the consul brave? **nonne fortis est consul?**
4. Do you hesitate to do that? **num dubĭtas id facĕre?**
5. Pray, what hinders you? **quid tandem te impĕdit?**
6. Is this law or the destruction of all laws? **haec utrum lex est an legum omnium dissolutio?**

7. Has he come? He has; **venitne? venit.**
8. Did the general lead out his army? He did not; **eduxitne imperātor exercĭtum? non eduxit.**
9. He inquired which states were in arms, **quaerēbat quae civitātes in armis essent.**
10. He inquires of the men themselves what the reason is, **quae causa sit ex ipsis quaerit.**
11. I asked whether he had arrived, **rogāvi pervenissetne.**
12. He asks whether they will come, **rogat num ventūri sint.**
13. The enemy were waiting (to see) whether our men would cross, **si nostri transīrent hostes exspectābant.**
14. The tribunes were not decided as to what they would do, **non satis tribūnis constābat quid agĕrent.**
15. Why, pray, should you fear? **quid tandem vereamĭni?**

VOCABULARY 16.

adopt, **insisto, ĕre, insti̇ti,** *no sup.*
ask, **rogo, āre, āvi, ātum.**
decided, be decided, determined, **satis constat,** *w. Dat. of person;* I am decided, determined, **satis mihi constat;** *lit.* it stands sufficiently firm for me.
find out, **reperio, īre, repĕri** or **reppĕri, repertum.**
how great, **quantus, a, um.**
inquire, **quaero, ĕre, quaesīvi** or **quaesii, quaesītum.**
island, **insŭla, ae,** *f.*
live, **vitam dego, ĕre, degi,** *no sup.*

or, **aut;** *in double questions,* **an:**[2]
or not, *in direct questions,* **an non;** *in indirect,* **necne.**
peril, be in peril, **in pericŭlo versor, āri, ātus sum.**
plan, **ratio, ōnis,** *f.*
please, **delecto, āre, āvi, ātum.**
pray, who pray? what pray? **quis tandem? quid tandem?**
size, **magnitūdo, ĭnis,** *f.*
whence, **unde;** *w. verbs of motion.*
where, **ubi;** *w. verbs of rest.*
whither, **quo;** *w. verbs of motion.*
whether, *in double indirect questions,* **utrum . . . . ne** (*enclitic*[2]): *in single indirect questions,* **num, si.**

EXERCISE 16.

1. Pray, who are you and where do you live? 2. Whence do you come and whither are you going? 3. What is there which can[3] now please you in this city? 4. Are

not these books worth reading⁴ a second time? 5. What, pray, hinders you from visiting⁵ me? 6. Has the general whom I saw in the city arrived? He has. ✓7. Do you hesitate to surrender yourself and all your property to me? I do not. ✓8. Will the French make peace with the Germans or make war upon them⁶? ✓9. The Germans are waiting (to see) whether the French will cross⁷ the river Rhine. 10. We shall ask these envoys whether they have come to see⁸ us. 11. They inquired of us⁹ how great was ¹⁰ the size of the island. ✓12. They can find out neither how great is the size of the island nor what tribes dwell (on it). ✓13. We are not decided (as to) what we shall do or what plan of battle we shall adopt. 14. Our friends asked us whether we would come to visit them or not. ✓15. When the soldiers found out in how great peril the camp and general were, they advanced to the attack.

Notes and Questions.

¹ Called also Dubitative or Doubting Questions; also Questions of Appeal.

² He asks whether you will go or stay, **rogat**,
{ utrum itūrus sis an remansūrus.
itūrusne sis an remansūrus.
itūrus sis an remansūrus.
itūrus sis remansūrusne.

³ *can*; what mood should be used? Why? See LN. X., REF. 1-9.

⁴ *Worth reading*; see LN. X., REF. 1-9, and EXAMPLES.

⁵ *from visiting*; see LN. X., REF. 13, 14, and EXAMPLES.

⁶ See REF. 6.

⁷ *Will cross*; in indirect questions referring to future time, the future active participle with the proper form of **esse** is generally used; see NOTE 2.

⁸ *to see*; what does this denote? What must be its construction?

⁹ *of us*; **quaero** is followed by **e, ex** or **a, ab** and Abl. of person; see Ex. 10.

¹⁰ *Was*; Indirect questions are subject to the same rules for sequence of tenses as Final and Consecutive Clauses: see LN. VII., REF. 1-7.

LESSON XVII.

THE INFINITIVE.

REFERENCES.

1, 2. *Subject of the Infinitive.* A. & G. 240 *f*: A. & S. 239: B. 225 RULE XVI.: B. & M. 1136: G. 341: H. 536.

1-5. *Infinitive as Subject.* A. & G. 270, *a;* NOTE immediately preceding 270: A. & S. 269 *coarse print:* B. 315, *a,* RULE LXXIII.: B. & M. 1118; 1147: G. 423; 535: H. 538.

6-10. *Infinitive without Subject-Accusative as Object or Complement.* A. & G. 271, NOTE, *a:* A. & S. 271: B. 315, *c,* RULE LXXIII.: B. & M. 1138: G. 424: H. 533, I., 1, 2.

EXAMPLES.

1. It was reported that *horsemen* were approaching, **nuntiātum est** *equĭtes* **accedĕre**.
2. *We* ought to measure out corn, *nos* **frumentum metīri oportet**.
3. You might have *given back* the hostages, **vobis obsĭdes** *reddĕre* **licuit**.
4. It pleased a part *to defend* the camp, **parti placuit castra defendĕre**.
5. They begged permission *to do* that, **petiērunt uti sibi id** *facĕre* **licēret**.
6. Gaul ought *to be* free, **libera debet** *esse* **Gallia**.
7. He hastens *to depart* from the city, **matūrat ab urbe** *proficisci*.
8. They dared *to cross* the river, **ausi sunt** *transīre* **flumen**.
9. They began *to fortify* a camp, **castra munīre coepērunt**.
10. Nobody could *see* an enemy, **hostem** *vidēre* **nemo potuit**.

How to express *can, could, may, might, ought, must.*

11. I can do this, **hoc facĕre possum**.
12. I could do this, **hoc facĕre potĕram** *or* **potuī**.
13. I could have done this, **hoc facĕre potuī**.

14. I may do this	mihi hoc facĕre licet.
	hoc faciam licet.
15. I might have done this .	mihi hoc facĕre licuit.
	hoc facĕrem licuit.
	hoc facĕre debeo.
16. I ought to do this	me hoc facĕre oportet.
	hoc faciam[1] oportet.
	hoc facĕre debui.
17. I ought to have done this	me hoc facĕre oportuit.
	hoc facĕrem[1] oportuit.
18. I must do this	me hoc facĕre necesse est.
	hoc faciam[1] necesse est.

VOCABULARY. 17.

able, be able, can, **possum, posse, potui.**
accustomed, be accustomed, be wont, **soleo, ēre, solĭtus sum.**
attempt, **conor, āri, ātus sum.**
begin, **incipio, cipĕre, cēpi, ceptum**; **coepi** and **coeptus sum, coepisse; coeptus sum** *only used w. pass. infin.*
dare, **audeo, ēre, ausus sum.**
determine, **statuo, ĕre, statui, statūtum.**
hasten, make haste, **matūro, āre, āvi, ātum.**
leave off, cease, **desĭno, ĕre, desīvi** or **desii, desĭtum.**
may, one may, it is allowed, it is permitted, **licet, licēre, licuit** or **licĭtum est.**
must, one must, it is necessary, it is unavoidable, **necesse est; necesse**, *an indecl. neut. adj.*
ought, one ought, it behooves, it is proper, **oportet, ēre, oportuit**; ought, be under obligation, **debeo, ēre, ui, ĭtum.**
prefer, wish rather, choose rather, **malo, malle, malui.**
report, **nuntio, āre, āvi, ātum.**
unwilling, be unwilling, not wish, **nolo, nolle, nolui.**
willing, be willing, wish, desire, **volo, velle, volui.**

EXERCISE 17.

1. We begged permission[2] to appoint a council of all Gaul. 2. The Gauls will beg permission to depart as soon as possible. 3. It has been reported that the French are making war upon the Swiss. 4. You ought to have exhorted the soldiers to fight[3] bravely. 5. Those soldiers

ought not to have prevented the enemy from cutting down[4] the bridge. 6. The French could have crossed the river yesterday but they cannot to-day. 7. You might have gone if you had been willing[5] to ask. 8. If you do not prefer to surrender yourselves and all your possessions, you must flee. 9. When our cavalry had begun[6] to advance, the enemy were fleeing. 10. Let us not[7] attempt to begin the battle on the left wing. 11. Our army is accustomed to delay in the vicinity of large towns for the sake of[8] supplies. 12. The infantry did not dare to cross the river, because it was[9] very wide and deep. 13. Do not hesitate[10] to cross the river, although it is wide and deep. 14. Pompey, since he was unwilling to flee, had determined to fight. 15. The governor hastened to go back into Italy as soon as possible. 16. Cease to fear that[11] the English will declare war against the Germans.

Notes and Questions.

[1] See A. & G. 331, c, f REMARK: A. & S. 273 4; 262 REM. 4: B. 295 REMARK: G. 559 REMARK: H. 501, I., 1; 502, 1.

[2] *We begged permission;* see Ex. 5.

[3] *to fight;* what does this denote and what must be its mood?

[4] *from cutting down;* see LN. X., REF. 10, 12.

[5] *if you had been willing;* what kind of a supposition? see LN. XII., REF. 1-5.

[6] *had begun;* see LN. XV., REF. 5-7.

[7] *not;* which negative should be used? See LN. V., NOTE 2.

[8] *for the sake of;* what must be the position of **causa**? See VY. 6.

[9] *because it was;* in this clause how would **quod** followed by the subjunctive differ in sense from **quod** followed by the indicative? See LN. XIV., NOTE 5.

[10] *do not hesitate;* how is a prohibition expressed in Latin? See LN. V., REF. 5-7.

[11] *fear that;* see LN. VIII., NOTE 8.

LESSON XVIII.

THE INFINITIVE (Continued).

REFERENCES.

1 - 6.^a *Infinitive with Subject-Accusative as Object.* A. &
G. 272, REMARK: A. & S. 270; 272: B. 315, *f*, 1–4: B. & M. 1148:
G. 527; 532; 533: H. 535, I.–III.
1 - 6.^b *Tenses of the Infinitive.* A. & G. 288, *a*, REMARK, *b*,
f: A. & S. 268 2: B. 317 REM. 4: B. & M. 1126–1129: G. 530: H.
537, NOTE, 3.
7, 8. *Predicate after Infinitive.* A. & G. 272 *a*, *b*: A. & S.
271 REM. 4: B. 225 REMARK: B. & M. 1142: G. 535 R. 2: H. 536 2,
1)–3).
9. *Historical Infinitive.* A. & G. 275: A. & S. 209 REM. 5,
NOTE 7: B. 315 *g*: B. & M. 1137: H. 536 1.

EXAMPLES.

1. He { says / thinks / believes / hopes / hears / rejoices } that the Gauls { have conquered, / are conquering, / will conquer, } { dicit / putat / credit / sperat / audit / gaudet } Gallos { vicisse. / vincĕre. / victūros (esse) or fore ut Galli vincant. }

2. He { said / thought / believed / hoped / heard / rejoiced } that the Gauls { had conquered, / were conquering / would conquer, } { dixit / putāvit / credĭdit / sperāvit / audīvit / gavīsus est } Gallos { vicisse. / vincĕre. / victūros (esse) or fore ut Galli vincĕrent. }

3. He ordered the third line to fortify the camp, **tertiam aciem castra munīre jussit.**
4. They do not permit wine to be imported, **vinum importāri non sinunt.**
5. I see that some one is absent, **video abesse non nemĭnem.**
6. They say that they will not return, **negant sese reversūros.**¹
7. I wish to be good, **volo esse bonus** *or* **volo me esse bonum.**
8. I may be good, **mihi bono esse licet.**
9. Caesar importuned the Aedui, **Caesar Aeduos flagitāre.**

VOCABULARY 18

accept, **accipio, cipĕre, cēpi, ceptum.**
already, **jam,** *adv.*
announce, **nuntio, āre, āvi, ātum.**
approach, **appropinquo, āre, āvi, ātum.**
believe, **credo, ĕre, credĭdi, credĭtum.**
denies, says not, **nego, āre, āvi, ātum.**
give back, **reddo, ĕre, reddĭdi, reddĭtum.**
hope, **spero, āre, āvi, ātum.**
lieutenant, **legātus, i,** *m.*
order, **jubeo, ēre, jussi, jussum.**
promise, **polliceor, ēri, pollicĭtus sum.**
recover, **recupĕro, āre, āvi, ātum.**
right, **jus, juris,** *n.*
terms, **condicio, ōnis,** *f.*
think, **puto, āre, āvi, ātum; arbĭtror, āri, ātus sum.**
tower, **turris, is,** *f.*; *acc. sing.* **turrim.**

EXERCISE 18.

1. The consul believes that the Gauls will neither send[1] envoys nor accept[1] any[2] terms of peace. 2. He hopes that the Aquitani have recovered their hostages and returned into their own country. 3. Our commander thinks that the Germans are marching into Switzerland in order that auxiliaries may not be sent from that nation into France. 4. The envoys said that they would report[3] these things to their friends and return to Caesar. 5. The lieutenant announced that the Germans were leading[4] a part of their troops across the river. 6. They promised that they would either give hostages or surrender themselves and all their possessions to the consul. 7. When the Gauls saw the tower approaching,[5] they sent legates to beg for[6] peace. 8. The consul began to march into those places in which he had heard that there were Germans. 9. He says that he ought not[7] to be hindered in his right by the Roman people. 10. He says that Ariovistus was not hindered from returning into Germany. 11. The general ordered his lieutenant to lead a part of his troops to the river and cut

down the bridge. 12. I shall ask whether he promised or not that he would give back the hostages. ✓13. There is no doubt that he thinks that we could have crossed[8] the river, although it was very deep and wide.

Notes and Questions.

[1] In Caesar's Commentaries the future active infinitive is very often written without **esse.**

[2] *any;* **alĭquam** or **ullam?** See Gen. Vy. under *"any."*

[3] *would report;* what is its time relative to the time of the principal verb *said?* What were the exact words of the envoys?

[4] *were leading;* what were the lieutenant's words? What tense of the infinitive must be used?

[5] *tower approaching = tower to approach.*

[6] *to beg for;* what is denoted by this infinitive and with what construction must it be rendered? See L<small>N</small>. VII., N<small>OTE</small> 1.

[7] *says . . . not;* Latin idiom, *denies.*

[8] *could have crossed;* compare L<small>N</small>. XVII., E<small>X</small>. 13.

LESSON XIX.

INDIRECT DISCOURSE.

Answer the following questions: What is a Direct Quotation? An Indirect? Direct Discourse or Oratio Recta? Indirect Discourse or Oratio Oblīqua? In Indirect Discourse, what mood is used in the principal clause of a declarative sentence? What mood in subordinate clauses? When Direct Discourse becomes Indirect, what changes are made in the pronouns? What verbs and expressions are followed by the Indirect Discourse?

For the answers consult the E<small>XAMPLES</small> and N<small>OTES</small> of this Lesson, and the following R<small>EFERENCES</small>: A. & G. 335, R<small>EMARK</small>; 336, *a;* also N<small>OTE</small> on pages 247, 248: A. & S. 266 2 w. preceding N<small>OTE</small>, R<small>EM</small>. 3: B. 316; 317, R<small>ULE</small> LXXIV.: B. & M. 1295; 1296, A., E., G., H., I.: G. 509 2; 651; 652; 653; 663, 1–4: H. 522, 1, 2; 513, I.-III.; 524; 526.

EXAMPLES.

Examples 1, 3, 5, 7 are Direct Discourse; 2, 4, 6, 8 are the same changed to Indirect Discourse.

1. He is hopeless with respect to that influence which he possesses, **de ea, quam habet, gratia despērat.**
2. Caesar finds that he is hopeless with respect to that influence which he possesses, **Caesar repĕrit illum de ea, quam habeat, gratia desperāre.**
3. I have not made war upon the Gauls, but the Gauls upon me, **non ego Gallis, sed Galli mihi bellum intulērunt.**
4. Ariovistus declared that he had not made war upon the Gauls, but the Gauls upon him, **Ariovistus praedicāvit non sese Gallis, sed Gallos sibi bellum intulisse.**
5. I wonder what business the Roman people have in my Gaul, which I have conquered, **mihi mirum vidētur, quid in mea Gallia, quam vici, populo Romāno negoti sit.**
6. Ariovistus answered that he wondered what business the Roman people had in his Gaul, which he had conquered, **Ariovistus respondit sibi mirum vidēri, quid in sua Gallia, quam vicisset, popŭlo Romāno negoti esset.**
7. Since he makes me this requital, this is what I demand of him, **quoniam hanc mihi gratiam refert, haec sunt, quae ab eo postŭlo.**
8. He said that since he made him this requital, this was what he demanded of him, **dixit quoniam hanc sibi gratiam referret, haec esse quae ab eo postulāret.**

VOCABULARY 19.

conquer, **vinco, ĕre, vīci, victum.**
demand, **postŭlo, āre, āvi, ātum;**
   I make this demand of him, **ab eo hoc postŭlo.**
especially, **praesertim,** *adv.*
find, **reperio, īre, repĕri** *and* **reppĕri, repertum.**
know, **scio, scire, scivi** *or* **scii, scitum.**
law, right, **jus, juris,** *n.*

manner, in what manner, **quemadmŏdum,** *adv.*
multitude, **multitūdo, ĭnis,** *f.*
on this side of, **cis,** *prep. w. Acc.*
private property, **res familiāris.**
reply, answer, **respondeo, ēre, respondi, responsum.**
requital, make requital, **gratiam refĕro, referre, retŭli, relātum;** I shall make you this re-

quital, **tibi hanc gratiam referam.**
rule over, **impĕro, āre, āvi, ātum,** w. *dat.*
settle, **consīdo, ĕre, sēdi, sessum.**
true, **verus, a, um.**
unoccupied, be unoccupied, **vaco, āre, āvi, ātum.**
with, at, near, at the house of, **apud,** *prep. w. acc.*

EXERCISE 19.

1. Caesar finds that Dumnorix always has about himself a large number of cavalry, and that he has increased his private property. 2. The envoy said he knew[4] that those things, which we had reported, were true. 3. The ambassador reported that all the rest of the Belgians were in arms, and that the Germans, who were dwelling on this side of the Rhine, had united themselves with these. 4. The king replied that he would not give back the hostages, which he had received, but[5] would make war upon the tribes who dwelt beyond the Alps. 5. Ariovistus answered that it was a law of war, that those, who had conquered, should in what manner they wished rule over[6] those whom they had conquered. 6. The general says that since they have made him this requital, he will make this demand of them, that they at once give back[7] the hostages. 7. The king thinks that since he has made you this requital, you ought not to demand that he give back the hostages. 8. The lieutenant reports that his general will make the Roman people this requital, provided they shall make[8] peace with him. 9. Caesar replies that no fields, which can be given especially to so great a multitude without wrong, are unoccupied in Italy; but they may settle, if they wish, in the territory of the Gauls, whose ambassadors are with him.

Notes and Questions.

[1] "When a statement is directly made, a question directly put, or a supposition directly expressed, the *language* is said to be direct, *oratio recta.*" *Roby.*

² "When a statement, question, or supposition is reported in a form which makes it dependent in construction on some such word as *said*, the language is said to be oblique or indirect (*oratio obliqua*)." *Roby*.

³ When Direct Discourse becomes Indirect, the forms of **ego** and **meus** are usually changed to those of **sui, suus, ipse** if they refer to the subject of the verb on which the Indirect Discourse is made dependent; otherwise to those of **is** or **ille**.

⁴ *knew;* which tense must be used? See Ln. XVIII., Ref. 1–6ᵇ.

⁵ *but;* "If a negative proposition is followed by an affirmative, in which the same thought is expressed or continued, **que, et,** or **ac**, is employed in Latin, where in English we use *but*." *Madvig*, 433, Obs. 2.

⁶ *should . . . rule over;* what would be the construction in Direct Discourse? See Ln. IX., Ref. 4–8.

⁷ *give back;* construction in Direct Discourse? See Ln. VIII., Ref. 1–14.

⁸ *provided they shall make;* see Ln. XII., Ref. 8.

LESSON XX.

INDIRECT DISCOURSE (*Continued*).

Answer the following questions: When Direct Discourse is made Indirect what does an indicative in the apodosis — conclusion — of a conditional sentence become? A subjunctive of the active voice? A subjunctive of the passive voice? What does an indicative in the protasis — conditional clause — become? Into what mood is an imperative changed? What mood does an interrogative sentence take? What changes are made in the tenses? For the answers consult the Examples of this lesson, the Table on page 54, and the following References: A. & G. 337, Note; 338, Remark; 339: A. & S. 266 2 Rem. 1, (*b*.), (*c*.), Rem. 4: B. 317, *a–d*: B. & M. 1296, A. — I.; 1303: G. 654–659: H. 523 II., 1, 2, III.; 527, I.–III.

EXAMPLES.

1. If he departs, I shall reward him, **si discessĕrit** (*fut. perf. ind.*), **ego illum remunerābor**.

2. He declares that if he departs, he will reward him, **praedĭcat si discessĕrit** (*perf. subj.*), **se illum remuneratūrum esse**.

3. He declared that if he should depart, he would reward him, **praedicāvit si discessisset, se illum remuneratūrum esse.**

4. If hostages should be given, I should make peace, **si obsĭdes dentur, pacem faciam.**

5. He answers that if hostages should be given, he would make peace, **respondet si obsĭdes dentur, pacem se esse factūrum.**

6. He answered that if hostages should be given, he would make peace, **respondit si obsĭdes darentur (dentur), pacem se esse factūrum.**

7. If hostages had been given, I should have made peace, **si obsĭdes dati essent, pacem fecissem.**

8. He answers, *or* he answered, that if hostages had been given, he would have made peace, **respondet,** *or* **respondit, si obsĭdes dati essent, pacem se fuisse factūrum.**

9. If I should make peace, hostages would be given, **si pacem faciam, obsĭdes dentur.**

10. He says that if he should make peace, hostages would be given, **dicit, si pacem faciat, futūrum esse,** *or* **fore, ut obsĭdes dentur.**

11. He said that if he should make peace, hostages would be given, **dixit, si pacem facĕret, futūrum esse,** *or* **fore, ut obsĭdes darentur.**

12. If I had made peace, hostages would have been given, **si pacem fecissem, obsĭdes dati essent.**

13. He says, *or* he said, that if he had made peace, hostages would have been given, **dicit,** *or* **dixit, si pacem fecisset, futūrum fuisse ut obsĭdes darentur.**

14. But if you persist, remember, **sin perseverābis, reminiscĕre.**

15. He said; but if he should persist, he must remember, **dixit, sin perseverāret, reminiscerētur.**

16. Let him engage in the contest when he wishes, **cum volet, congrediātur.**

17. He answered that he might engage in the contest when he wished, **respondit, cum vellet, congrederētur.**

18. If I am willing to forget, can I lay aside memory? **si oblivisci volo, num memoriam deponĕre possum?**

19. He answered; if he should be willing to forget, could he lay aside memory? **respondit; si oblivisci vellet, num memoriam deponĕre posse?**

TABLE showing the Changes made in Moods and Tenses when Direct Discourse becomes Indirect.

I. Moods.

1. Principal Clauses: Statements.

Direct Discourse.		Indirect Discourse.
Indicative	becomes	*Infinitive.*
Active Subjunctive in the apodosis of a conditional sentence	becomes	*Future Active Participle* with **esse** or **fuisse.**
Passive Subjunctive in the apodosis of a conditional sentence	becomes	**fore,** or **futūrum esse** or **fuisse,** with **ut** and the *subjunctive.*

2. Principal Clauses: Questions.

Indicative, 1st or 3d person,	becomes	*Infinitive.*
Indicative, 2d person,	becomes	*Subjunctive.*
Subjunctive.	remains	*Subjunctive.*

3. Principal Clauses: Commands or Prohibitions.

Imperative	becomes	*Subjunctive.*
Subjunctive.	remains	*Subjunctive.*

4. Subordinate Clauses of All Kinds.

Indicative	becomes	*Subjunctive.*
Subjunctive.	remains	*Subjunctive.*

II. Tenses.

1. When an Indicative or a Subjunctive of Direct Discourse passes into a Subjunctive of Indirect Discourse.

Present } *Future* }	become	*Present,* often *Imperfect,* when made dependent upon a Principal Tense; *Imperfect,* sometimes *Present,* when made dependent upon an Historical Tense.
Perfect } *Future-Perfect* }	become	*Perfect,* often *Pluperfect,* when made dependent upon a Principal Tense; *Pluperfect,* sometimes *Perfect,* after an Historical Tense.
Imperfect	remains	*Imperfect.*
Pluperfect	remains	*Pluperfect.*

2. When an Indicative of Direct Discourse passes into an Infinitive of Indirect Discourse.

Present	remains	*Present.*
Future or *Future-Perfect*	becomes	*Future Participle* with **esse.**
Perfect } *Imperfect* } *Pluperfect* }	become	*Perfect.*

VOCABULARY 20.

danger, **perĭcŭlum, i,** *n.*
declare, **praedīco, āre, āvi, ātum.**
disturb, **perturbo, āre, āvi, ātum.**
entire, **totus, a, um.**
forget, **obliviscor, i, oblītus sum.**
high-born, **nobĭlis, e.**
kill, **interficio, ficĕre, fēci, fectum.**

manner, in no ordinary manner, **non mediocrĭter,** *adv.*
pleasing, **gratus, a, um.**
prepared, **parātus, a, um.**
reward, **remunĕror, āri, ātus sum.**
try, **experior, īri, expertus sum.**
understand, **intellego, ĕre, lexi, lectum.**

EXERCISE 20.

Translate sentences 1-6 into Indirect Discourse, making 1, 3, 5 dependent upon **dicit,** and 2, 4, 6, upon **dixit.**

1. If the Gauls who dwell on this side of the Alps depart,[1] the Romans will reward them. 2. You are the only person who has ever led[2] troops across the Rhine. 3. If the Gauls had staid in Italy, there could have been no friendship between them and me.[3] 4. If you wish to conquer, wheel about and advance fearlessly into the enemy's country. 5. Can I forget that this is my native country and that I am the consul of these people[4]? 6. While Caesar was delaying[5] in the vicinity of Geneva for the sake of supplies, such fear suddenly seized the entire army that it disturbed the minds of all in no ordinary manner. 7. He declared that if they wished to try a second time, he was prepared to fight a second time. 8. Ariovistus replied, that if he should kill Caesar, he would do a favor[6] to many high-born men among the Roman people.[7] 9. The king answered, that if we had surrendered our town to him, his private property would have been greatly increased. 10. He said that he understood with how great danger you had done[8] that. 11. He says that if we had not come, the enemy would have cut down the bridge.

Notes and Questions.

[1] *depart;* which tense should be used in Direct Discourse and which in Indirect? See Ex's 1 and 2.

[2] *has led;* what mood is necessary in Direct Discourse? See Ln. X., Ref. 1-9 and Ex. 7.

[3] *between them and me ;* translate as if it read, *for me with them.*

[4] *people;* is it necessary to translate this word?

[5] *was delaying;* what tense would be used in Direct Discourse? See Ln. VI., Ref. 2.

[6] *a favor;* **gratum.**

[7] *among the Roman people;* render by the *genitive.*

[8] *you had done;* what mood would be necessary in Direct Discourse? See Ln. XVI., Ref. 9-14.

LESSON XXI.

THE GENITIVE.

REFERENCES.

1-3. *Subjective Genitive with Nouns.* A. & G. 214, *a, g:* A. & S. 211, Rem. 2, Rem. 3 (*b.*): B. 232, Rule XXI., Rem. 1-3: B. & M. 751; 753; 756: G. 361, 1: H. 396, I., II.

3-6. *Limited Word Omitted.* A. & G. 214 *b:* A. & S. 211 Rem. 7: B. 230 Rem. 2: B. & M. 755: G. 360, Rem. 3: H. 398.

7-12. *Subjective Genitive with Verbs.* A. & G. 214 *c, d:* A. & S. 211 Rem. 8, (1)-(3): B. 230, Rem. 1: B. & M. 780: G. 365, Rem. 1-3: H. 401, Notes 2, 3; 402.

EXAMPLES.

1. The fear of the people, the running together of all the good, the faces and looks of these, **timor popŭli, concursus bonŏrum omnium, horum ora vultusque.**

2. For the sake of aid, **auxili causa.**

3. Is unpopularity *caused by severity* very much more to be dreaded than *that* caused by negligence? **num est vehementius** *severitātis* **invidia quam nequitiae pertimescenda?**

4. *For the purpose of* avoiding suspicion, **suspiciōnis vitandae,** *sc.* **causa.**

5. Quintus, *son* of Marcus, **Quintus Marci**, *sc.* **filius.**
6. With respect to my danger and *that* of the state, **de meo perĭcŭlo et rei publĭcae,** *sc.* **perĭcŭlo.**
7. It is the part of wisdom to see, **sapientiae est vidēre.**
8. It is the duty of the consul, **consŭlis est.**
9. It is your duty to care for the state, **vestrum est rei publĭcae providēre.**
10. It was foolish to think of peace, **erat amentis pacem cogitāre.**
11. The fifth class consists of murderers, **quintum genus est parricidārum.**
12. I shall grant that the fault belongs to Ligarius, **confitēbor culpam esse Ligari.**

VOCABULARY 21.

avert, drive away, **depello, ĕre, depŭli, depulsum.**
care for, **provideo, ēre, vīdi, vīsum,** *w. dat.*
criminal, **facinorōsus, i,** *m.*
decide, **decerno, ĕre, crēvi, crētum.**
desolation, **vastĭtas, ātis,** *f.*
destruction, **exitium, i,** *n.*
establish, **constituo, ĕre, ui, ūtum.**
foolish, stupid, **amens,** *gen.* **amentis.**
highest, **summus, a, um.**
house, **tectum, i,** *n.*
it is the duty, part of, **est** *w. pred. gen.*
misfortune, **calamĭtas, ātis,** *f.*

never, **numquam (nunquam),** *adv.*
retain, hold, **teneo, ēre, ui, tentum.**
separate, **sejungo, ĕre, junxi, junctum.**
state, **res publĭca, rei publicae,** *f.*
troubled, anxious, **sollicĭtus, a, um.**
welfare, prosperity, **salus, ūtis,** *f.*
whole, on the whole, **universus, a, um.**
wisdom, **sapientia, ae,** *f.*
wise, **sapiens,** *gen.* **sapientis.**
withdraw, **deficio, ficĕre, fēci, fectum;** to withdraw from allegiance to the king, **a rege deficĕre.**

EXERCISE 21.

1. Cicero said that Catiline was bringing to destruction and desolation the temples of the immortal gods and lives[1] of all the citizens. 2. Catiline was hindered by Cicero from bringing[2] to destruction and desolation the houses of

the city. 3. Those men, who have withdrawn from allegiance to the state, ought[3] never to retain the rights of citizens. ✓4. Cicero said that they, who had withdrawn[4] from allegiance to the state, had never in the city of Rome retained the rights of citizens. ✓5. The orator saw that the senators were troubled not only with respect to their danger and that[5] of the state, but also, if that should be averted,[6] with respect to his. ✓6. It is the duty of the senate to care for the highest welfare of the state. 7. Do not doubt[7] that it is[8] your duty[9] to care for the state. 8. It is the part of wisdom to see that the misfortunes[1] of many citizens cannot be separated from that[5] of the state. 9. The consul says that the fifth class consists of criminals. 10. Cicero said that the colonies, which Sulla had established in Etruria, consisted on the whole of very good citizens and very brave men. ✓ 11. There is no doubt that it was foolish[10] to think of peace when the enemy was already in the city. ✓12. It will be wise[10] to delay in the vicinity of this town for the sake of aid. ✓13. The consul said that the senate ought fearlessly to decide with respect to its own highest welfare and that of the Roman people. 14. Let us at once carefully and fearlessly decide[11] with respect not only to our own welfare but also to that of the Roman people.

Notes and Questions.

[1] *lives;* the Latin often has a noun in the singular number where the English requires the plural.

[2] *from bringing;* what constructions may depend upon verbs of hindering? See L_N. X., R_EF. 10–12 and 13, 14.

[3] *ought;* see L_N. XVII., Examples 16, 17.

[4] *had withdrawn;* what mood must be used in a subordinate clause of Indirect Discourse? See L_N. XIX.

[5] *that;* see R_EF, 3–6 and E_X. 6.   [6] *should be averted;* pluperf. subj.

[7] *do not doubt;* how is a prohibition expressed in Latin? See L_N. V., R_EF. 5–7.

⁸ *that it is;* what construction usually depends upon a negative clause expressing or implying doubt? See Ln. X., Ref. 10-12.

⁹ *your duty;* instead of the predicate genitive of a *personal* pronoun, the nominative or accusative of the *possessive* is generally used: see Ex. 9.

¹⁰ With adjectives of one ending the genitive masculine, instead of the nominative or accusative neuter, is generally used in a predicate after **esse** to avoid ambiguity; e. g. *it is wise,* **sapientis est** (*it is of a wise man*).

¹¹ *Let us . . . decide;* see Ln. V., Ref. 3, 4.

LESSON XXII.

THE GENITIVE (*Continued*).

REFERENCES.

1-3. *Objective Genitive.* A. & G. 217: A. & S. 211 Rem. 2, (*a.*)–(*c.*), Rem. 3: B. 233, Rule XXII.: B. & M. 751; 753: G. 361, 2; 362: H. 396, III.

4, 5, 12. *Constructions used instead of Objective Genitive.* A. & G. 217 Rem., *a:* A. & S. 211 Rem. 2 (*d.*): H. 396 Note 1.

6-8. *Partitive Genitive.* A. & G. 216, *a*, 1-4: A. & S. 212: B. 227 Rule XVII., *a–g* B. & M. 771; 772: G. 366-371: H. 397 1-4.

9. *Constructions used instead of Partitive Genitive.* A. & G. 216 *c*, *d:* A. & S. 212 Rem. 2 Note 4: B. 227 Rem. 2: B. & M. 775: G. 371 Rem. 5: H. 397 Note 3.

10. *When the Partitive Genitive is not to be used.* A. & G. 216 *e:* A. & S. 212 Rem. 2 (5) *last part:* B. 227 Rem. 3: G. 368 Rem. 2: H. 397 2 Note.

EXAMPLES.

1. The destruction of the commonwealth, **perniciem rei publicae.**

2. From dangers to the commonwealth, **a rei publĭcae pericŭlis.**

3. A leader in the war, **dux belli**; preparation for war, **comparatio belli.**

4. By the love of the gods for you, **deōrum erga vos amōre.**
5. With danger to himself, **suo pericŭlo.**
6. Which *of us* do you think knows not what *plan* you adopted? **quid** *consili* **cepĕris quem** *nostrum* **ignorāre arbitrāris?**
7. There is no one who does not contribute as much *good-will* as he can, **est nemo, qui non tantum, quantum potest, confĕrat** *voluntātis.*
8. No one of these, **horum nemo;** sufficient garrison, **satis praesidi;** some place, **alĭquid loci;** one of whom, **quorum alter;** where in the world are we, **ubinam gentium sumus?** the bravest of the soldiers, **milĭtum fortissĭmi.**
9. One of the sons, **unus e filiis.**
10. The welfare of all of us, **salūtem omnium nostrum.**
11. There is not one slave, **servus est nemo.**
12. With respect to the destruction of all of us, **de nostro omnium**[1] **interĭtu.**

VOCABULARY 22.

as much ... as, **tantus ... quantus.**
bestow, **impertio, īre, īvi** or **ii, ītum;** *w. acc. of direct object and dat. of indirect.*
contribute, devote, **confĕro, conferre, contŭli, collātum.**
due, be due, **debeor, ēri, debĭtus sum.**
endeavor to bring about, **molior, īri, ītus sum.**
forgetting, forgetfulness, **oblivio, ōnis,** *f.*
former, **vetus,** *gen.* **vetĕris.**
garrison, protection, **praesidium, i,** *n.*
plot, **cogĭto, āre, āvi, ātum.**
preparation, **comparatio, ōnis,** *f.*
renown, **gloria, ae,** *f.*
save, **conservo, āre, āvi, ātum.**
sufficiently, sufficient, **satis,** *adv.*
surely, **profecto,** *adv.*
the one ... the other, **alter ... alter.**

EXERCISE 22.

1. Do not doubt that the leader of the enemy is in the senate, endeavoring to bring about the destruction of the commonwealth. 2. No one can prevent the commander of that camp from endeavoring to bring about[2] the destruction of the commonwealth. 3. There were in that most dignified council of the earth, those who were plotting[3]

with respect to the destruction of all¹ of us. 4. Provided my destruction is separated⁴ from dangers to the commonwealth, I shall not be unwilling to die.⁵ 5. The city has been saved by the highest love of the immortal gods for you, but with danger to me. 6. All of us desire to know who will be⁶ leaders in this war. 7. There was not one slave who did not contribute to the common welfare⁷ as much good-will as he dared and as he could. 8. Cicero said that he would bestow⁸ upon Lucullus as much praise as was due to a brave man and great commander. 9. There is no doubt that the general devoted all the remaining time, not to forgetting the former war, but to preparation for a new. 10. Who of us⁹ does not know what protection the city has?¹⁰ 11. There is no one of these who does not know¹¹ that the city has sufficient garrison. 12. There will surely be some place for my renown amid the praises for this man. 13. Two kings were captured, of whom one had slaughtered the bravest of our soldiers, the other had murdered one of my sons.

Notes and Questions.

¹ **omnium**; "A possessive in any case may have a genitive in apposition." A. & G.

² *from endeavoring to bring about;* see LN. X., REF. 10-12.

³ *were plotting;* see LN. X., REF. 1-9.

⁴ *is separated;* see LN. XII., REF. 8.

⁵ *I shall not be unwilling to die;* see LN. II., REF. 10-12.

⁶ *will be;* how should it be expressed? See LN. XVI., NOTE 7.

⁷ *to the common welfare;* **ad w. acc.**

⁸ *would bestow;* what mood and tense must be used? See LN. XVIII., REF. 1-6ᵇ.

⁹ *of us;* see LN. III., NOTE 2.

¹⁰ *has;* see LN. XVI., REF. 9-14.

¹¹ *does not know;* see LN. X., REF. 10-12.

LESSON XXIII.

THE GENITIVE (Continued).

REFERENCES.

1-5. *Genitive of Quality.* A. & G. 215, *a-c:* A. & S. 211 Rem. 6, (5); 214, Rem. 1: B. 238; Rule XXVII., Rem. 1-5: B. & M. 757; 758; 799; 800: G. 364, Remark; 378: H. 396 V.; 404, Notes 1, 2; 405.

6-12. *Genitive with Adjectives.* A. & G. 218, *a-d:* A. & S. 213, Rem. 1; 222 Rem. 2 (*b.*): B. 234, Rule XXIII., 1-3, Rem. 1-3: B. & M. 765; 767; 776: G. 373; 374: H. 399, I., 1-3, II.

EXAMPLES.

1. In a contest of such a kind, **in ejus modi certamine.**
2. Rocks of great weight, **magni ponderis saxa.**
3. All which is of such a character, **quae sunt omnia ejus modi.**
4. The depth of the river was about *three feet*, **fluminis erat altitudo circiter** *pedum trium.*
5. It is *worth while* for me, **est mihi** *tanti.*
6. Mindful of you, **memorem vestri.**
7. Unacquainted with affairs, **ignarus rerum.**
8. Very skilful in wars, **bellorum peritissimus.**
9. Like the truth, **veri simile.**
10. Peculiar to Caesar, **proprium Caesaris.**
11. Not sharing in renown, **expers gloriae.**
12. He is made participant in the public council, **fit publici consili particeps.**

VOCABULARY 23.

anxiety, **sollicitudo, Inis,** *f.*
beyond, more than, **praeter,** *prep. w. acc.*
decide, adjust, **dijudico, āre, āvi, ātum.**
eager for, **appětens,** *gen.* **appetentis.**
exile, **exsilium (exilium), i,** *n.*
fond, loving, **amans,** *gen.* **amantis.**
full, **plenus, a, um.**
greedy, **avidus, a, um.**
help, **succurro, ěre, curri, cursum,** *w. dat.*
like, **similis, e.**

massacre, **internecio, ōnis,** *f.*
narrow, small, **parvus, a, um.**
of such a kind, of such a character, **ejus modi;** *often written* **ejusmŏdi.**
on account of, **propter,** *prep. w. acc.*
participant, **partĭceps,** *gen.* **particĭpis.**
rouse, incite, **inflammo, āre, āvi, ātum.**
skilful, practically acquainted with, **perītus, a, um.**

submit to, endure, **subeo, īre, ii, ĭtum,** *w. acc.*
the other, **cetĕrus, a, um;** *pl.*, the rest.
unacquainted with, ignorant, **ignārus, a, um.**
unfortunate, **miser, misĕra, misĕrum.**
unpopularity, **invidia, ae,** *f.*
zeal, **studium, i,** *n.*

EXERCISE 23.

1. The soldiers could not be prevented from hurling rocks of great weight. 2. Would that all my fellow-citizens were[1] men of great valor. 3. The depth of the river, which we crossed, was said to be about nine feet. 4. All of us seem to be of so narrow a mind that we think[2] all things will perish at one and the same time with ourselves. 5. That war was of such a kind that it ought to have roused your minds to the highest zeal. 6. All those quarrels were of such a character that they were decided by a massacre of citizens. 7. It is worth while for me to submit to unpopularity, provided Catiline goes[3] into exile. 8. It would be worth while for me to submit to unpopularity, if only Catiline would go into exile.[4] 9. The Romans more than the other nations were always eager for glory and greedy for praise. 10. No one can be found so like you that he will not go into exile. 11. There is no doubt that all of us are very fond of leisure. 12. Since no one is unacquainted with trouble, all ought to know how to help the unfortunate. 13. It is said that Caesar[5] was practically acquainted with the arts not only of peace, but also of war. 14. This man hopes to be made[6] participant in the council of his nation. 15. When we were waging

war, we were full of anxiety on account of love for our country.[7]

Notes and Questions.

[1] *would ... were;* what mood and what tenses are used to express a wish that cannot be fulfilled? See LN. V., REF. 8, 9.

[2] *that we think;* what must be the construction of this clause? Is it used adverbially or substantively? See LN. IX.

[3] *goes;* what mood is necessary after **dum modo**.

[4] What kind of a supposition is expressed by this sentence? To what time does it refer? What mood and tense must be used?

[5] *It is said that Caesar;* the Latin prefers the personal construction: *Caesar is said.*

[6] *to be made;* **fore ut fiat.**

[7] *for our country;* see LN. XXII., REF. 1-3.

LESSON XXIV.

THE GENITIVE (Continued).

REFERENCES.

1-3. *With Verbs of Memory.* A. & G. 219, REMARK: A. & S. 216; 218: B. 235, RULE XXIV., REM. 1: B. & M. 788; 793: G. 375: H. 406 II.; 409, I.; 410, I., 1, 2.

4-8. *With Verbs of Emotion.* A. & G. 221, *a–c:* A. & S. 215, NOTE 3: B. 237, RULE XXVI., REM. 1, 2: B. & M. 783; 805: G. 376: H. 406 I.; 409 III.

9, 10. *With Verbs of Judicial Action.* A. & G. 220, *a, b:* A. & S. 217: B. 236, RULE XXV.: B. & M. 793: G 377: H. 409 II.; 410 III.

11. *With Verbs of Plenty and Want.* A. & G. 223: A. & S. 220, 3: B. & M. 910: G. 389 REM. 2: H. 410 V., 1.

12-14. *With* refert *and* interest. A. & G. 222, *a:* A. & S. 219, REMARK: B. 237 NOTE: B. & M. 809; 810: G. 381; 382: H. 406 III.; 408, I.–IV.

EXAMPLES.

1. I remember your constancy, **memĭni constantiae tuae.**
2. Forget murder, **obliviscĕre caedis.**
3. He was reminding us of his extreme poverty, **admonēbat nos egestātis.**
4. Pity such labors, **miserēre labōrum tantōrum.**
5. We pity them, **eōrum nos misĕret.**
6. Do not pity your brothers, **cave te fratrum misereat.**
7. The Athenians repented of the act, **facti Athenienses paenituit.**
8. Of what should I be ashamed? **me quid pudeat?**
9. He was accused of treason, **accusātus est proditiōnis.**
10. He was condemned for treason in his absence, **absens proditiōnis damnātus est.**
11. I need your counsel, **indigeo tui consili.**
12. It is of great importance to Cicero, **magni Cicerōnis intĕrest.**
13. It matters little to me what you say, **parvi mea refert quid dicas.**
14. Who is there to whom it is important that this law remain? **quis est cujus intersit istam legem manēre?**

VOCABULARY 24.

absent, in one's absence, **absens,** *gen.* **absentis.**
accuse, **accūso, āre, āvi, ātum.**
ashamed, something causes one to be ashamed, **pudet, pudēre, puduit** *or* **pudĭtum est;** I am ashamed, **me pudet.**
condemn, **damno, āre, āvi, ātum.**
inactivity, **inertia, ae,** *f.*
it is of importance, it concerns, it matters, **intĕrest, esse, fuit.**
kindness, **beneficium, i,** *n.*
military affairs, **res militāris.**
need, **indigeo, ēre, ui,** *no sup.*
negligence, **nequitia, ae,** *f.*
old, **senex,** *gen.* **senis.**
pity, **misereor, ēri, miserĭtus sum; misĕret, miserēre, miseruit,** *impers.*
poor, **pauper,** *gen.* **paupĕris.**
remember, **memĭni, isse.**
remind, admonish, **admoneo, ēre, ui, ĭtum.**
repent, **paenĭtet, paenitēre, paenituit.**
sound, **sanus, a, um.**
treason, **proditio, ōnis,** *f.*

EXERCISE 24.

1. Do not forget me and that I am your consul. 2. We ought to forget others'[1] faults, but remember our own. 3. Pity the sorrows of a poor old man. 4. It is of great importance to a general to be practically acquainted with military affairs and to have brave soldiers. 5. It is of little importance to me whether he comes to visit[2] you or not.[3] 6. I fear that he will remind me of my negligence and inactivity. 7. There is no doubt that we have been accused of treason in our absence. 8. Cicero said that he condemned himself for inactivity and negligence. 9. All of us hope that you will not be condemned[4] for treason. 10. The consul says that he will never repent[5] of his acts. 11. Magistrates were not ashamed to come into this place, since our ancestors had adorned[6] it with the spoils of fleets. 12. Of what should we be ashamed[7] when we have done all we can?[8] 13. All ought to pity those who do not pity themselves. 14. There is no doubt that every one needs a sound mind and a sound body. 15. If Caesar should repent[9] of his kindness, this man would be condemned for treason.

Notes and Questions.

[1] *others'*; render with the possessive adjective **aliēnus, a, um**.

[2] *to visit*; see L.N. VII., Ref. 10–11.

[3] *or not*; how should it be expressed in an indirect question? See Vy. 16.

[4] *will not be condemned*; "The future infinitive is often expressed by **fore (futūrum esse) ut** with the subjunctive — necessarily where there is no supine stem." A. & G.

[5] *will . . . repent*; see Note 4.

[6] *had adorned*; see L.N. XIV., Ref. 1–5, and Ex. 5.

[7] *should we be ashamed*; see L.N. XVI., Ref. 15.

[8] *all we can*; the relative is rarely omitted in Latin.

[9] *If . . . should repent*; what kind of a supposition?

LESSON XXV.

THE DATIVE CASE.

REFERENCES.

1-3. *With Transitive Verbs.* A. & G. 225, c, e: A. & S. 223: B. 240, Rule XXVIII.: B. & M. 818; 819: G. 344: H. 382; 384, II., 1)-3).

4, 5. *Double Construction.* A. & G. 225 d: G. 348: H. 384 II., 2.

6-11. *With Intransitive Verbs.* A. & G. 226; 227, a, e: A. & S. 223 Rem. 2; 225: B. 241 Rule XXIX.; 244 Rule XXXII.: B. & M. 831; 824: G. 345: H. 384, I.; 385, I., II., Note 3.

12, 13. *Dative or Accusative according to Signification.* A. & G. 227 c: B. & M. 836: G. 347 H. 385 II. 1.

14, 15. *When "to" and "for" are to be rendered by* ad *and* pro. A. & G. 225 b; 236 Remark: G. 344 Remark: H. 384 3, 1), 2).

EXAMPLES.

1. To you our country stretches out her hands, **vobis manus tendit patria.**
2. No destruction will be prepared for the city, **nulla pernicies moenĭbus comparabĭtur.**
3. Death, with which they threaten me, **mors, quam mihi minitantur.**
4. He presented books to me, **libros mihi donāvit.**
5. You presented your clerk with a ring, **scribam tuum anŭlo donasti.**
6. If this has happened to no one, **si hoc contĭgit nemĭni.**
7. Nor could I persuade myself, **nec mihi persuadēre potĕram.**
8. It was necessary to obey the senate, **parēre senatui necesse erat.**
9. Cease to spare me, **mihi parcĕre desinĭte.**
10. They chose to serve the Roman people rather than to rule over others, **servīre popŭlo Romāno quam imperāre aliis maluērunt.**

11. We seem to do enough for the republic, **satisfacĕre rei publĭcae vidēmur.**
12. If you consult me, *or* if you ask my advice, **si me consŭlis.**
13. Consult for yourselves, *or* consult your interests, **consulĭte vobis.**
14. I wrote a letter to Pompey, **littĕras ad Pompēium scripsi.**
15. They used to speak for liberty, **pro libertāte loquebantur.**

VOCABULARY 25.

angry, be angry, **irascor, i, irātus sum.**
choose rather, prefer, **malo, malle, malui.**
consult, ask advice of, **consŭlo, ĕre, consului, consultum,** *w. acc.; w. dat.*, consult for, consult the interests of.
crime, **scelus, scelĕris,** *n.*
decree of the senate, **senātus consultum.**
drive out, **ejicio, ejicĕre, ejēci, ejectum.**
except, **praeter,** *prep. w. acc.*
for, in behalf of, **pro,** *prep. w. abl.*
happen, **contingit,** *pf.* **contĭgit.**
intrust, **commendo, āre, āvi, ātum.**

obey, **pareo, ēre, ui, ĭtum.**
pardon, **ignosco, ĕre, ignōvi, ignōtum.**
please, **placeo, ēre, ui, ĭtum.**
pray, beseech, **quaeso, ĕre, īvi** *or* **ii, ĭtum.**
present, **dono, āre, āvi, ātum.**
rule over, command, **impĕro, āre, āvi, ātum.**
satisfy, do enough, **satisfacio, facĕre, fēci, factum.**
serve, **servio, īre, īvi** *or* **ii, ītum.**
threaten, **minĭtor, āri, ātus sum.**
truth, **verum, i,** *n.*
write, **scribo, ĕre, scripsi, scriptum.**

EXERCISE 25.

1. Our country intrusts to you the temples of her gods and the lives of her citizens. 2. They threatened my brother with the severest punishment that they might drive him out into exile. 3. If this should happen to me, I should choose to go into exile rather than to obey the decree of the senate. 4. They could not persuade themselves to go[1] into exile. 5. These men are angry with me because I have driven out[2] their brother into exile.

6. Our ancestors chose to rule over themselves rather than to serve a king. 7. The decree of the senate pleased me so very much that I wrote[3] a letter to my brother with respect to it. 8. Pardon me, I pray, if I speak the truth freely. 9. May the gods pardon[4] all your crimes, the senate can not. 10. All exhorted me to consult[5] for my own life and welfare. 11. You ought to consult the interests of those men in their absence, since they are your fellow-citizens. 12. Let the consul ask the advice of the senate (as to) whether he ought[6] to drive out this man into exile or not. 13. Our orators speak more fearlessly than they fight for their country. 14. He presented his son with many books, worthy to be read[7] a second time. 15. They thought that they would satisfy the city, if they should avoid the suspicion of fear.

Notes and Questions.

[1] *to go;* see L*n*. VIII., R*ef*. 1–14.

[2] *because I have driven out;* what moods may be used after **quod** and with what difference in signification? See L*n*. XIV., R*ef*. 1–5, and N*ote* 5.

[3] *that I wrote;* what is expressed by this clause? What must be its construction? See L*n*. IX., R*ef*. 1–3.

[4] *may ... pardon;* see L*n*. V., R*ef*. 8, 9.

[5] *to consult;* see N*ote* 1.

[6] *whether he ought;* what kind of a question? What must be its mood?

[7] *worthy to be read;* see L*n*. X., R*ef*. 1–9.

LESSON XXVI.

THE DATIVE (*Continued*).

REFERENCES.

1 - 7. *With Compounds.* A. & G. 228, *a, b*; 229, *b*: A. & S. 224, R*em*. 1, 2, 4: B. 242, R*ule* XXX., R*em*. 3: B. & M. 824; 826: G. 346: H. 386, 2.

8-11. *Of the Possessor.* A. & G. 231, REMARK, *a*, *b*, *c:* A. & S. 226, REM. 1: B. 243, RULE XXXI., NOTE: B. & M. 821: G. 349; 322: H. 387, NOTE. 1.

12. *Of the Agent.* A. & G. 232 *a*, *c:* A. & S. 225 H.: B. 247, RULE XXXV.: B. & M. 844: G. 352: H. 388 1.

13, 14. *How Intransitive Verbs are used in the Passive.* A. & G. 230: B. & M. 453: G. 208: H. 465 1.

EXAMPLES.

1. I withstood you by my own efforts, **per me tibi obstĭti.**
2. This day you will prefer to the greatest manifestations of joy for you, **hunc tu diem tuis maximis gratulationĭbus antepōnes.**
3. The senate would have laid violent hands on me, **mihi senātus vim et manus intulisset.**
4. He met me, **se mihi obvium tulit.**
5. I went to meet you, **ego tibi obviam ivi.**
6. Take this fear from me, **hunc mihi timōrem erĭpe.**
7. We wrested the sword from his hands, **ei ferrum e manĭbus extorsĭmus.**
8. The gates have no keeper, **nullús est portis custos.**
9. Marcellus has me as witness, **Marcello sum testis.**
10. They said that Cethegus had had a dispute with the rest, **Cethēgo cum cetĕris controversiam fuisse dixĕrunt.**
11. His name is Caesar, **ei Caesări nomen est,** *or* **ei nomen Caesár est,** *or* **ei nomen Caesăris est.**
12. I see that war has been undertaken by me, **mihi bellum susceptum esse video.**
13. When they wished no one to be pardoned, **cum ignosci nemĭni vellent.**
14. I am envied, you are envied, he is envied, **mihi invidētur, tibi invidētur, ei invidētur.**

VOCABULARY 26.

controversy, dispute, **controversia, ae,** *f.*
disturbance, **tumultus, us,** *m.*
effort, by his own efforts, **per se.**
envy, **invideo, ēre, vīdi, vīsum.**
fertile, **opīmus, a, um.**
force, **vis, vis,** *f.*; by force, **per vim.**
fruitful, **fertĭlis, e.**
lay violent hands on, **vim et manus infero, inferre, intŭli, illātum.**

meet, **se obvium ferre;** go to
meet, **obviam** (*or* **obvius, a,
um**) **eo, ire, ivi, itum.**
neighbors, **finitĭmi, ōrum,** *m. pl.*
prefer, **antepōno, ĕre, posui,
positum.**
protection, **praesidium, i,** *n.*
provision, make provision, **provideo, ēre, vīdi, vīsum.**

rage, madness, **furor, ōris,** *m.*
surpass, **antecello, ĕre,** *no perf.
nor sup.*
take from, **eripio, eripĕre, eripui,
ereptum.**
very much, **vehementer,** *adv.*
withstand, thwart, **obsto, āre,
obstĭti, obstātum.**
witness, **testis, is,** *m. and f.*

EXERCISE 26

1. We withstood your villainy and rage by our own efforts. 2. Do not hesitate[1] to thwart this man's villainies and madness by your own efforts. 3. They would choose[2] to lay violent hands[3] on this man rather than to bring war upon their country. 4. We prefer this day to all the spoils of war that we have been able to take. 5. Our fields are so fertile and fruitful that they surpass the fields of our neighbors. 6. They met us in a forest when we were making[4] a journey through Switzerland. 7. If you come to visit me, I shall go to meet you. 8. They took this money from us by force that they might make war upon their country. 9. We have very many books, which are not worth reading[5] at all. 10. If we had had[6] this dispute with the rest, we should not have pardoned them. 11. The king would be very much envied, if the Romans should present[6] him this city.[7] 12. This man said that his name was Marcellus and that he should make a journey into Italy. 13. You have me as witness that Catiline could[8] not persuade you to make war upon your country. 14. Cicero said that provision had been made by him that the city might have sufficient protection without any disturbance. 15. If we should make war upon the state, we should not be envied,[9] but should be condemned for treason.

Notes and Questions.

¹ *do not hesitate;* how may a prohibition be expressed? See LN. V., REF. 5-7.

² *would choose;* see A. & G. 265: A. & S. 260 II.: B. 293, III.: B. & M. 1177: G. 250: H. 485.

³ *violent hands;* what is *Hendiadys?* A. & G. page 298: A. & S. 323 2 (3): B. 370 *b* 2: B. & M. 1379 2d: G. 695: H. 636 III. 2.

⁴ *we were making;* see A. & G. 325: A. & S. 263 5 **REM. 2:** B. 304: B. & M. 1244: G. 581, II.: H. 521, II., 2.

⁵ *which are not worth reading at all;* Latin idiom, *not at all worthy which (so that they) are read;* for the construction see LN. X., REF. 1-9 and EX. 9.

⁶ What kind of a supposition is expressed in sentence 10? What in sentence 11?

⁷ *him this city;* what are the different constructions for these words? See LN. XXV., REF. 4, 5.

⁸ *that Catiline could;* accusative and infinitive depending upon **testis**, which has the force of a declarative verb.

⁹ *we should not be envied;* see REF. 13, 14 and EXAMPLES.

LESSON XXVII.

THE DATIVE (*Continued*).

REFERENCES.

1-3. *Two Datives.* A. & G. 233: A. & S. 227, REM. 2, 3: B. 246, RULE XXXIV.: B. & M. 848: G. 350: H. 390, I., II.

4-7. *With Adjectives.* A. & G. 234, *a:* A. & S. 222, 3, REM. 1: B. 245, RULE XXXIII.: B. & M. 860; 862: G. 356: H. 391, I.

8, 9. *Other Constructions with Adjectives.* A. & G. 234, *b, c,* REMARK, *e:* A. & S. 222 REM. 2 (*b.*), REM. 4: B. 245 REM. 1-3: B. & M. 863; 865: G. 356 REM. 1-5: H. 391 II., 1-4.

10, 11. *Of Reference or Interest.* A. & G. 235: B. 244, RULE XXXII.: H. 384 II. 2).

EXAMPLES.

1. Whose affairs ought to be a care to you, **quorum res vobis curae esse debent.**

2. Whom have you protected with your fleets? **cui praesidio classĭbus vestris fuistis?**
3. Who bring you enjoyment, **qui vobis fructui sunt.**
4. My country is dear to me, **patria mihi cara est.**
5. Most unfriendly to you, **inimicissĭmi vobis.**
6. Your good-will is pleasant to me, **est mihi jucunda vestra voluntas.**
7. I think him very like a god, **eum simillĭmum deo judĭco.**
8. Who are fit for friendship, **qui ad amicitiam sunt idonei.**
9. I thought that it was my duty to keep the army as near as possible to the enemy, **esse officium meum putāvi exercĭtum habēre quam proxĭmum hostem.**
10. The sight of Cethegus hovers before my eyes, **versātur mihi ante ocŭlos aspectus Cethēgi.**
11. For you alone has the murder of many citizens been unpunished, **tibi uni multōrum civium neces impunītae fuērunt.**

VOCABULARY 27.

agreeable, **gratus, a, um.**
ally, **socius, i,** *m.*
annoying, **molestus, a, um.**
can not but, **facĕre non possum quin,** *w. subj.*
care, **cura, ae,** *f.*
comitium, **comitium, i,** *n.*
dear, **carus, a, um.**
defendant, **reus, i,** *m.*
enjoyment, **fructus, us,** *m.*
forbearance, **venia, ae,** *f.*
near, **prope,** *adv.;* nearest, **proxĭmus, a, um.**

safety, **salus, ūtis,** *f.*
stand, **sto, stāre, stĕti, stătum.**
suited, **accommodātus, a, um.**
threaten, **immineo, ēre,** *no perf. nor sup.*
unfriendly, **inimīcus, a, um.**
voice, **vox, vocis.**
weapon, **telum, i,** *n.*
protection, **praesidium, i,** *n.;* to protect any one, **alicui praesidio esse.**

EXERCISE 27.

✓1. If my voice has been a means of safety for any one,¹ surely I ought to be pardoned.² ✓2. If the general had protected the city with his troops, he would not have been condemned for treason. ✓3. I can not but think that this province has brought great enjoyment to the Roman people. 4. We fear that this army will not be³ a great protection to the Roman people. 5. Their⁴ country, temples, and gods were very dear⁵ to all the Romans. 6. Cicero asked Catiline whether the light could⁶ be agreeable to him, when he knew⁷ that there was no one⁸ of the senators who did not know⁹ that he had stood⁸ in the comitium with a weapon. 7. He said that the commonwealth ought to be a very great care to us. 8. Cicero did not think that many could be found who were fit for friendship. 9. He besought the judges to grant¹⁰ him forbearance, suited to the defendant and not annoying to them. 10. Two kings, most unfriendly not only to you but also to your allies and friends, have now for a long time been threatening¹¹ entire Asia. 11. It is the general's duty¹² to keep both the infantry and cavalry as near as possible to our city. 12. Our ancestors both acquired much territory and waged many wars for us. 13. I can not but think that fear of this man will hover continually before your mind.

Notes and Questions.

¹ *means of safety for any one* = *for safety to any one.*

² *to be pardoned;* see LN. XXVI., REF. 13, 14.

³ *will not be;* see LN. VIII., NOTE 8.

⁴ *their;* see LN. IV., REF. 1-8.

⁵ *very dear;* see LN. II., REF. 6-8.

⁶ *could;* see LN. XVI., REF. 9-14, and LN. XVII., EX. 12.

⁷ *when he knew;* cum w. subj. because there is an accessory notion of cause.

⁸ *there was no one; he had stood;* see LN. XVIII., REF. 1-6ª and 1-6ᵇ.

⁹ *who did not know;* see LN. X., REF. 1-9.

¹⁰ *to grant;* see LN. VIII., REF. 1-14.

¹¹ *have . . . been threatening;* see LN. VI., REF. 3.

¹² *It is the general's duty;* see LN. XXI., REF. 7-12 and Examples.

LESSON XXVIII.

THE ACCUSATIVE.

REFERENCES.

1-3. *Direct Object.* A. & G. 237, a: A. & S. 229: B. 212, RULE VII.; 213: B. & M. 712: G. 329: H. 371; 464, I., II.

4-8. *With Verbs which in English require a Preposition.* A. & G. 237 b, c.: A. & S. 229 REM. 2; 232 (2); B. & M. 716; 717: G. 329 REM. 1: H. 371 III. NOTE 1.

9-11. *With Compounds.* A. & G. 237 d; 228 a: A. & S. 233, (1)–(3): B. 215, a, 1, 2, b: B. & M. 718; 719: G. 330: H. 372.

12-15. *Cognate.* A. & G. 238: A. & S. 232: B. 214, a, b: B. & M. 713: G. 331: H. 371 I., 2, 1), II.

EXAMPLES.

1. Defend the name and welfare of the Roman people, **popŭli Romāni nomen salutemque defendĭte.**
2. I hope the gods will requite me as I deserve, **spero deos mihi ac mereor relatūros esse gratiam.**
3. You have thanked me, **mihi gratias egistis.**
4. Honors, which they despair of, **honōres, quos despērant.**
5. Citizens grieved for my misfortune, **cives meum casum doluērunt.**
6. I shudder greatly at the annoyance, **vexatiōnem perhorresco.**
7. Catiline breathing out crime, **Catilīnam scelus anhelantem.**
8. They do not complain of this as much as they fear it, **non tam hoc queruntur quam verentur.**
9. Citizens who stand about the senate, **cives qui circumstant senātum.**
10. They crossed the river, **flumen transiērunt.**
11. They approached me, **me adiērunt.**
12. You seem to have won a victory, **victoriam vicisse vidēris.**
13. He has fought battles, **pugnāvit proelia.**

14. What should I reply? *or* What reply should I make? **quid respondeam?**

15. All have one and the same opinion, **omnes sentiunt unum atque idem.**

VOCABULARY 28.

as, **atque, ac,** *conj.*
as much ... as, **tam ... quam.**
boldness, **audacia, ae,** *f.*
deserve, **mereor, ēri, merĭtus sum.**
despair of, **despēro, āre, āvi, ātum.**
ditch, **fossa, ae,** *f.*
feel, think, have opinion, **sentio, īre, sensi, sensum.**
feel thankful, **gratiam**[1] **habeo.**
go to, approach, **adeo, īre, īvi** *or* **ii, ĭtum.**
grieve for, **doleo, ēre, ui, ĭtum.**
live, **vivo, ĕre, vixi, victum.**
question, **quaestio, ōnis,** *f.*

rampart, **vallum, i,** *n.*
requite, **gratiam**[1] **refĕro, referre, retŭli, relātum.**
shudder greatly at, **perhorresco, ĕre, perhorrui,** *no sup.*
stand about, around, **circumsto, āre, stĕti, stătum.**
surround, put around, **circumdo, āre, dĕdi, dătum.**
thank, **gratias**[1] **ago, ĕre, egi, actum.**
the same ... as, **idem ... qui.**
wretch, **scelerātus, i,** *m.*
win a victory, **victoriam vinco, ĕre, vīci, victum.**

EXERCISE 28.

1. We ought to hope that all the gods will requite[1] us as we deserve. 2. The senate thanked the consul in very strong terms because he had driven out[2] that wretch into exile. 3. We cannot but think that we ought to surround the city with a rampart and a ditch.[3] 4. Let us not stand about the senate, but let us go to the consul and ask his advice.[4] 5. They inquired of us[5] whether we despaired of the city's safety. 6. There was not one slave who did not shudder greatly at[6] the boldness of citizens. 7. There is no doubt that the citizens grieved very much for the misfortune of the state. 8. They were not wont to complain[7] of this as much as they feared it, that Catiline would go[8] into exile. 9. We did not doubt that you had fought a

great battle and won a great victory. 10. What reply should I make to the envoys if they should ask my advice? 11. If they had asked my advice, I should have made the same reply as you made. 12. Since there is no one who does not know⁹ that you did not grieve for the misfortune of the commonwealth, what reply will you make? 13. This is the only question in respect to which all citizens have one and the same opinion.¹⁰ 14. While I live¹¹ I shall feel thankful to you for that which you have done for me. 15. Provided you go to the consul and ask¹² his advice, I shall thank you in strong terms.

Notes and Questions.

1 Observe that **gratia** is always in the *plural* with **agĕre**; with **referre** and **habēre** mostly in the *singular;* that they take the dative of the person *whom* one *thanks,* ETC.; and **pro** with the ablative of that *for which* one *thanks,* ETC.

2 *had driven out;* what mood should be used? See L.N. XIV., NOTE 5.

3 *city . . . ditch;* see L.N. XXV., REF. 4, 5.

4 *ask his advice;* see L.N. XXV., REF. 12, 13, and EXAMPLES.

5 *of us;* see L.N. XVI., NOTE 9.

6 *who did not shudder greatly at;* see L.N. X., REF. 1–9.

7 *wont to complain;* see L.N. VI., REF. 4–6, and EX. 6.

8 *that Catiline would go;* accusative and infinitive, appositive with **hoc.**

9 *who does not know;* see NOTE 6.

10 *have . . . opinion;* see NOTE 6.

11 *while I live;* what time is denoted and what tense must be used?

12 *go and ask;* see L.N. XII., REF. 8.

LESSON XXIX.

THE ACCUSATIVE (*Continued*).

REFERENCES.

1-4. *Two Accusatives of the same Person or Thing.* A. & G. 239, a; A. & S. 230: B. 216, RULE VIII.: B. & M. 715; G. 334; H. 373.

LATIN PROSE COMPOSITION.

5-10. *Two Accusatives — Person and Thing.* A. & G. 239 c, REMARK, d: A. & S. 231: B. 217, RULE IX., REM. 1-3: B. & M. 734; 738: G. 333, REM. 2: H. 374, NOTES 1-4.

11, 12. *Two Accusatives with Compound Verbs.* A. & G. 239 b: A. & S. 233, (1): B. 215 b: B. & M. 718 2 d: G. 330 REM. 1: H. 376.

13-15. *Limit of Motion.* A. & G. 258, b: A. & S. 237, REM. 4: B. 221, RULE XII.: B. & M. 938; 943: G. 410: H. 380, I., II., 2, 1).

EXAMPLES.

1. The people elected Marius consul, **Marium consŭlem popŭlus creāvit.**
2. Marius was elected consul by the people, **Marius consul a popŭlo creātus est.**
3. You have made the senate firmer, **senātum firmiōrem fecistis.**
4. Jupiter, whom we call the preserver of this city, **Juppĭter, quem statōrem hujus urbis nomināmus.**
5. The consul asked Silanus his opinion, **consul Silānum sententiam rogāvit.**
6. Silanus, the first to be asked his opinion, **Silānus, primus sententiam rogātus.**
7. He teaches boys rudiments, **puĕros elementa docet.**
8. I shall teach him to be silent, **docĕbo eum tacēre.**
9. Let them teach him what sort of a man Roscius was, **doceant eum qui vir Roscius fuĕrit.**
10. I advise them as follows, **eos hoc moneo.**
11. Whom Caesar had led across the Rhine, **quos Caesar traduxĕrat Rhenum.**
12. He ascertained that the Belgians had been led across the Rhine, **reperiēbat Belgas Rhenum esse traductos.**
13. He will betake himself to Marseilles, **se Massiliam confĕret.**
14. Men go into the country, **rus homĭnes eunt.**
15. He asked the Gauls why they had come to his house, **quaesīvit a Gallis quam ob rem domum suam venissent.**

VOCABULARY 29.

advise, **moneo, ēre, ui, ĭtum.**
call, name, **appello, āre, āvi, ātum; nomĭno, āre, āvi, ātum.**
choose, **delĭgo, ĕre, lēgi, lectum.**
country, **rus, ruris,** *n.*; **rus** *is country as contrasted with* **urbs**

faithful, **fidēlis, e.**
hold, **teneo, ēre, ui, tentum.**
home, homeward, **domum.**
Latin, speak Latin, **Latīne loquor, i, locūtus sum.**
opinion, **sententia, ae,** *f.*
rudiments, **elementa, ōrum,** *n. pl.*
set out, **proficiscor, i, profectus sum.**

stupid, **stultus, a, um.**
suitable, fit, proper, **idoneus, a, um.**
teach, show, **doceo, ēre, ui, doctum.**
tried, proved, **probātus a, um.**

EXERCISE 29.

1. The Roman people could have elected Catiline consul, but they wished to condemn him for treason. 2. Marcellus ought to have been elected consul, but the people accused him of treason in his absence. 3. There was no one so stupid as not to see[1] that you had made the senate better. 4. This man, whom we call our friend and ally, is suitable to be sent[2] as ambassador to the Belgians. 5. Silanus, the first to be asked his opinion because he had been elected consul, decided that punishment ought to be inflicted upon those who were held in custody. 6. I should be glad to teach[3] you to speak Latin, if only I could speak Latin myself. 7. He says that I ought to have shown the judges what sort of a man the defendant was.[4] 8. We advise our fellow-citizens as follows :[5] let them not stand about the senate nor despair of the commonwealth. 9. When the general was informed that the Belgians had already led a part of their troops across the Rhine, he set out with three legions and came to that part which had not yet crossed the river. 10. Catiline's friends reported that he,[6] having been driven out into exile, would betake himself[7] to Marseilles. 11. Let us ask the envoys why they went home and not to Geneva. 12. The gates have no keeper, let us go into the country. 13. He sent money to Ephesus to him[8] whom you chose out of all your friends as the most tried and faithful.

Notes and Questions.

[1] *as not to see;* cf. L<small>N</small>. IX., N<small>OTE</small> 1.
[2] *suitable to be sent;* see L<small>N</small>. X., R<small>EF</small>. 1-9, and E<small>X</small>. 8.
[3] *I should be glad to teach;* see L<small>N</small>. II., R<small>EF</small>. 10-12.
[4] *was;* what mood is necessary and why?
[5] *as follows;* **hoc.** [6] *he;* see L<small>N</small>. IV., R<small>EF</small>. 1-8.
[7] *he . . . would betake himself;* what would these words be in Direct Discourse?
[8] *to him;* express in Latin, *I sent to him; I gave to him; I wrote to him.*

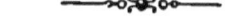

LESSON XXX.

THE ACCUSATIVE (*Continued*).

REFERENCES.

1-6. *Adverbial.* A. & G. 240, *a, b:* A. & S. 231 R<small>EM</small>. 5: B. 222, R<small>ULE</small> XIII.: B. & M. 731: G. 331, R<small>EM</small>. 3: H. 378, 2.

7. *Of Specification.*[1] A. & G. 240 *c*, N<small>OTE</small>: A. & S. 234 II.: B. 218, R<small>ULE</small> X., R<small>EMARK</small>: B. & M. 728: G. 332: H. 378, 1.

8. *In Exclamations.* A. & G. 240 *d:* A. & S. 238 2: B. 223, R<small>ULE</small> XIV.: B. & M. 725: G. 340: H. 381.

9-13. *Of Time and Space.* A. & G. 240 *e:* A. & S. 236: B. 220, R<small>ULE</small> XI.: B. & M. 950; 958: G. 335-338: H. 379.

EXAMPLES.

1. Why are you silent? **quid taces?**
2. What reason is there why we should doubt? **quid est quod dubitēmus?**
3. You have very great influence, **vales plurĭmum.**
4. Have the countenances of these moved you in no respect? **nĭhilne te horum ora movērunt?**
5. I had foretold that they would come *at that* time, *id* **tempŏris eos ventūros praedixĕram.**
6. They live for the most part upon milk, **maxĭmam partem lacte vivunt.**
7. Like a god in countenance and shoulders, **os humerosque deo simĭlis.**

8. O wretched state! **O condiciōnem misĕram!**
9. You are sixty years old, **annos sexaginta natus es.**
10. More than forty years old, **annos natus major quadraginta.**
11. He has had a residence at Rome many years, **domicilium Romae multos annos habuit.**
12. Throughout these years, **per hosce annos.**
13. Zama is five days' journey from Carthage, **Zama quinque diērum iter a Carthagĭne abest.**

VOCABULARY 30.

about, **circĭter,** *adv.*
acorn, **glans, glandis,** *f.*
always, **semper,** *adv.*
band, **manus, us,** *f.*
countenance, **os, oris,** *n.*
day, **dies, diēi,** *m.*
dissolve, **dimitto, ĕre, mīsi, missum.**
flesh, **caro, carnis,** *f.*
have power, influence, **valeo, ēre, ui, ĭtum;** to have very great influence, **plurĭmum valēre.**
milk, **lac, lactis,** *n.*
night-guard, **nocturnum praesidium.**
old, **natus, a, um.**
pace, **passus, us,** *m.*; **mille passus,** a mile.
to be feared, **pertimescendus, a, um,** *fut. pass. part.*
wait for, **praestōlor, āri, ātus sum,** *w. dat.*

EXERCISE 30.

✓ 1. Why should I urge you,[2] by whom men have already been sent forward to Marseilles, that they may wait for you in the vicinity of that city? 2. Cicero asked Catiline whether the night-guard of the Palatine had in no respect moved him. 3. The case itself speaks and that[3] always has very great influence. 4. What reason is there why we should hesitate[4] to delay a few days in the vicinity of Marseilles for the sake of aid? 5. It is said that our ancestors lived for the most part upon acorns and milk. 6. Although Caesar was in the senate at that time, he came home because the senate had been dissolved. 7. There is no doubt that this boy resembles[5] his father in countenance. 8. O war greatly to be feared, since its leader will have[6] this band of wretches! 9. Cicero was sixty-four years old when he was murdered.⁷ 10. I am fifty years old; how old are you? I am more than sixty. 11. While the enemy were delaying⁸ many days for the sake of supplies, we marched fifty miles into their country. 12. They did not doubt that our army had protected the province⁹ of Sicily many years. 13. The consul sent forward scouts, who were to choose¹⁰ a place suitable for a camp, about six hundred paces from the enemy.

Notes and Questions.

¹ Also called "Greek Accusative," and "Synecdochical Accusative."

² *why should I urge you?* What kind of question? See Ln. XVI., Ref. 15.

³ *and that;* **quae.**

⁴ *we should hesitate;* see Ln. X., Ref. 1-9.

⁵ *resembles = is like.*

⁶ *will have;* see Ln. IX., Note 4, *last part.*

⁷ *when he was murdered;* see Ln. XXVI., Note 4.

⁸ *were delaying;* see Ln. VI., Ref. 2.

⁹ *had protected the province;* see Ln. XXVII., Ref. 1-3.

¹⁰ *who were to choose;* see Ln. VII., Note 1.

LESSON XXXI.

THE ABLATIVE.

REFERENCES.

1-3. *Of Separation.* A. & G. 243, *a-e:* A. & S. 251: B. 256, Rule XLI.: B. & M. 916; 907; 923: G. 388-390: H. 413; 414.

4. *Of Source.* A. & G. 244, *a:* A. & S. 246: B. 255, Rule XL.: B. & M. 918: G. 395: H. 413; 415, II.

5-10. *Of Cause.* A. & G. 245, *b, c:* A. & S. 247, 1, (1), (2), Rem. 1, 2: B. 257, Rule XLII., Rem. 1-3: B. & M. 873: 875: G. 406; 407, Rem. 1: H. 416, Note 1.

11. *Of Agent.* A. & G. 246, *b:* A. & S. 248, I.: B. 260, Rule XLV.: B. & M. 878: G. 403: H. 415, I.

EXAMPLES.

1. Free the republic from fear, **libĕra rem publĭcam metu.**
2. He resigned the magistracy, **magistrātu se abdicāvit.**
3. We were without harbors, **portŭbus carebāmus.**
4. Apollo was born of Jupiter and Latona, **Apollo Jove natus est et Latōna.**
5. By my order, **meo jussu.**
6. By a decree of the senate, **senātus consulto.**
7. Exult because of your robbery, **exsulta latrocinio.**
8. Who shine in purple, **qui fulgent purpŭra.**
9. No one is happy who lives in accordance with that law, **beātus est nemo qui ea lege vivit.**
10. While they were pleased with their estates, **dum praediis delectantur.**
11. He was not driven out by me, **a me non ejectus est.**

VOCABULARY 31.

ally, **socius, i,** *m.*
appoint, **constituo, ĕre, ui, ūtum.**
born, be born, descended, **nascor, i, natus sum.**
be without, deprived, **careo, ēre, ui, ĭtum.**
blockade, **obsidio, ōnis,** *f.*
deprive, **privo, āre, āvi, ātum.**
exult, run riot, **exsulto, āre, āvi, ātum.**
find, **reperio, īre, repĕri** and **reppĕri, repertum.**

free, release, relieve, **libĕro, āre, āvi, ātum.**
harbor, **portus, us,** *m.*
invite, **invīto, āre, āvi, ātum.**
moment, **punctum, i,** *n.*
order, by order, **jussu,** *abl. sing. masc.*
pirate, **praedo, ōnis,** *m.*
please, **delecto, āre, āvi, ātum.**
resign, **abdĭco, āre, āvi, ātum;** *w. acc. of pers. pron. and abl. of that which one resigns.*

EXERCISE 31.

1. Cicero said that if Catiline had staid in the city, although they would have withstood[1] all his plans, nevertheless they would never have freed the republic from peril. 2. Let Metellus be considered a distinguished man, since he twice released his city from blockade and the fear of slavery. 3. The senator does not think that those who

have attempted to deprive us all of life, ought to live a moment of time. 4. If you had compelled the defendant to resign the praetorship, the senate would have thanked you in very strong terms. 5. Two citizens were found who relieved[2] you of this care, and promised that they would murder me in my bed. 6. We fear that[3] for many years[4] our country will be not only without provinces but also without harbors. 7. It was said[5] that Caesar was descended from Trojan blood. 8. Caesar did not think that death had been appointed by the immortal gods for the purpose of punishment. 9. He asked the senators how many cities of the allies they supposed had either been taken by the pirates or abandoned because of fear. 10. Let us live in accordance with the laws that we may not[6] go into exile by order of the consul. 11. They asked me why I was so pleased with the dwellings and temples of their city. 12. Let him exult by reason of his crimes, that he may seem not[6] to have been driven out by me to strangers but invited to his friends. 13. Do not run riot because of your great crimes, but resign your office at once, go to the temples of the immortal gods, and beg for pardon.[7]

Notes and Questions.

[1] *would have withstood;* what mood is used in a subordinate clause of indirect discourse?

[2] *who relieved;* i. e. of such a character that they relieved; what mood is necessary? What use of that mood?

[3] *that;* how should it be rendered after a verb of fearing?

[4] *for many years;* what case is used to express duration of time?

[5] *It was said;* see LN. XXIII., NOTE 5.

[6] *that . . . not;* how expressed in a final clause? See LN. IX., NOTE 3.

[7] *beg for pardon;* translate as if it read, *beg that they pardon you.*

LESSON XXXII.

THE ABLATIVE (Continued).

REFERENCES.

1. *Of Manner.* A. & G. 248, REMARK: A. & S. 247, 2: B. 259, RULE XLIV., REMARK: B. & M. 873; 876: G. 401, REMARK: H. 419, III., NOTE 2.

2, 3. *Of Accompaniment.* A. & G. 248 a: A. & S. 249 III., REMARK: B. & M. 874: G. 391, REM. 1: H. 419, I., 1, 1).

4, 5. *Of Means and Instrument.* A. & G. 248 c: A. & S. 247, 3; 249: B. 258, RULE XLIII.: B. & M. 873: G. 403: H. 420.

6-8. *With certain Deponents.* A. & G. 249: A. & S. 245: B. 258, a: B. & M. 880: G. 405: H. 421, I.

9-11. *With certain Adjectives.* A. & G. 245 a; 254 b: A. & S. 244: B. 257: B. & M. 919: G. 373 REM. 1-4: H. 421, III.

EXAMPLES.

1. They think that they will perish with less pain, **minōre dolōre peritūros se arbitrantur.**

2. He began to follow with all his troops, **cum omnĭbus copiis sequi coepit.**

3. He was following close after with all his troops, **subsequebātur omnĭbus copiis.**

4. Not yet do I wound those with my voice who ought to be slain with the sword, **quos ferro trucidāri oportēbat, eos nondum voce vulnĕro.**

5. Large multitudes of the enemy were destroyed in many battles, **magnae hostium copiae multis proeliis sunt delētae.**

6. My voice has performed its duty, **mea vox officio functa est.**

7. Enjoy fortune and renown, **fruĕre fortūna et gloria.**

8. Whose service I make use of, **quorum opĕra utor.**

9. You said that you were satisfied with the murder of us who had staid, **te nostra, qui remansissēmus, caede contentum esse dicēbas.**

10. Trusting to you I shall defend your right, **fretus vobis vestrum jus defendam.**

11. Prisons worthy the crime of desperate men, **custodias dignas scelere hominum perditōrum.**

VOCABULARY 32.

butcher, slay, **trucīdo, āre, āvi, ātum.**
darkness, **tenebrae, ārum,** *f. pl.*
deservedly, **merĭto.**
destroy, **deleo, ēre, ēvi, ētum.**
guards, **custodiae, ārum,** *f. pl.*
hide, **obscūro, āre, āvi, ātum.**
hostile, **infestus, a, um.**
impious, **nefarius a, um.**
justly, **jure.**
long since, **jam pridem,** *adv.*
night-attack, **nocturnus impĕtus.**

pain, **dolor, ōris,** *m.*
perform, **fungor, i, functus sum.**
satisfied, **contentus, a, um.**
service, **opĕra, ae,** *f.*
sword, **gladius, i,** *m.*
take possession of, **occŭpo, āre, āvi, ātum.**
trusting to, **fretus, a, um.**
use, make use of, employ, **utor, uti, usus sum.**
unjustly, **injuriā.**
watches, **vigiliae, ārum,** *f. pl.*

EXERCISE 32.

1. We took possession of Marseilles by a night-attack, before you were able to protect that city with garrisons, guards, and watches. 2. I could not understand why they thought that they would die with less pain in company with many than (they would) if¹ they should die alone. 3. If I were unjustly accused by my fellow-citizens, I should choose² to go into exile rather than to be seen by the hostile eyes of all. 4. Let us hasten with all our troops to the enemy's camp and take possession of it by a night-attack. 5. The enemy, because they remembered our former victory,³ could not be prevented from butchering our soldiers with their swords. 6. I cannot but think that we shall destroy large multitudes of the enemy in many battles. 7. This wretch, who ought long since to have been led to death, has been attempting to lay waste the whole earth with fire and sword. 8. What (reason) is

there why⁴ you should stay longer in this city, when you know that the night with its darkness can not hide your impious crimes? 9. You will never repent of having performed⁵ your duty to your country.⁶ 10. The senate deservedly and justly thanked the praetors because their service, which I had employed, was fearless and faithful.⁷ 11. We feared that they would not be satisfied with the punishment of you who had staid⁸ in the city. 12. The enemy trusting to the large number of their troops attacked us vigorously.

Notes and Questions.

¹ *than . . . if*; see L̄n. XII., Ref. 6.

² *If I were . . . accused, . . . I should choose*; what kind of a supposition? To what time does it refer? See Ln. XII., Ref. 1–5.

³ *victory*; what case do verbs of memory govern?

⁴ *what reason is there why*; see Ln. XXX., Ex. 2, and Ln. X., Ref. 1–9.

⁵ *of having performed*; render with the perfect infinitive.

⁶ *to your country*; see Ln. XXII., Ref. 1–3.

⁷ *because . . . faithful*; translate as if it read, *because I had employed their fearless and faithful service.*

⁸ *had staid*; see Ln. XIV., Ref. 6.

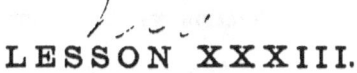

LESSON XXXIII.

THE ABLATIVE (*Continued*).

REFERENCES.

1-3. *With Comparatives.* A. & G. 247, *a*, Remark, *b*: A. & S. 256, 2, Rem. 1, 4, 9: B. 261, *c*, Rem. 1, 3: B. & M. 895; 899; 902: G. 399: H. 417, 1, Note 1.

4-6. *Construction with* Plus, *etc.* A. & G. 247 *c*: A. & S. 256 Rem. 6: B. 261 Rem. 2: B. & M. 900: G. 311 Rem. 4: H. 417, Note 2.

7-9. *Measure of Difference.* A. & G. 250, Remark: A. & S. 256 Rem. 16: B. 262 Rule XLVII.: B. & M. 929: G. 400: H. 423.

10, 11. *Of Quality*.[1] A. & G. 251, *a*: A. & S. 211 Rem. 6, (3): B. 263 Rule XLVIII., Note: B. & M. 888; 759: G. 402, Rem. 1: H. 419, II., 2, 1)-4).

EXAMPLES.

1. Who (was) more illustrious than Themistocles? **quis clarior Themistocle?**

2. What can be said (that is) more reasonable than this request? **quid hac postulatiōne dici potest aequius?**

3. This evil has spread more widely than we think, **latius opiniōne dissemiātum est hoc malum.**

4. When he had been sick more than a year, **cum plus annum aeger fuisset.**

5. You are more than sixty years old, **amplius annos sexaginta natus es.**

6. Catiline had not more than two thousand soldiers, **Catilīna non amplius duōbus milībus milĭtum habuit.**

7. My country is much dearer to me than my life, **patria mihi vita mea multo est carior.**

8. You came a little while ago into the senate, **venisti paulo ante in senātum.**

9. The less certain the life of man is, the more ought the state to enjoy the life of an eminent man, **quo minus certa est homĭnum vita, hoc magis res publĭca frui debet summi viri vita.**

10. You exhort him to be of good courage, **jubes eum bono esse anĭmo.**

11. A man of such moderation, **vir tanta temperantia.**

VOCABULARY 33.

acquire, **consĕquor, i, secūtus sum.**
ago, a little while ago, **paulo ante.**
compassion, **misericordia, ae,** *f.*
evidence, **testimonium, i,** *n.*
influence, **auctorĭtas, ātis,** *f.*
just, fair, reasonable, **aequus, a, um.**
kindness, **humanĭtas, ātis,** *f.*
long, longer, longest, **diu, diutius, diutissĭme,** *refers to time.*
mild, **mitis, e.**
praise, **laus, laudis.**
request, demand, **postulatio, ōnis,** *f.*
savageness, **atrocĭtas, ātis,** *f.*
spread, **dissemĭno, āre, āvi, ātum.**
the ... the, **quanto ... tanto, quo ... eo** *or* **hoc.**
widely, **late,** *adv.*

EXERCISE 33.

1. Because the consul[2] was not moved by savageness of heart but by kindness and compassion, he asked the senate who was milder than himself. 2. Who of the Romans was more illustrious than Cicero, who more powerful than Caesar? 3. What could we have asked that was more just than this request? 4. There is no doubt that this evil has spread more widely than any one supposes. 5. If the Swiss had not had more than five thousand soldiers, we should have put them to flight. 6. This man was considered worthy of the highest praise, because he had often said[3] that his country was much dearer to him than his life. 7. There is no doubt that the men who stand about[4] the senate and whose voices you could have heard[4] a little while ago, are more fearless than you. 8. The more severe the siege was, the more numerous were the letters and messengers that were sent[5] to Caesar. 9. This man is of such kindness and courage that the longer he stays with us the happier we are. 10. Why ought this man, who is already more than eighty years old, to be led to death by order of the consul? 11. If we did not have less than a thousand infantry, we should take possession of that city by a night-attack. 12. I have always been of such a mind as to think that nothing could be better than friendship. 13. Although these wretches are of a better disposition than part[6] of the soldiers, nevertheless they will be put to death with the sword. 14. Let this general have everlasting fame,[7] because he has twice freed our city from blockade and the fear of slavery.

Notes and Questions.

[1] *Ablative of Quality*; also called *Ablative of Characteristic*; *Ablative of Description*.

[2] *consul:* put this word in the principal clause.

³ *because he had often said;* what mood should be used and why?

⁴ *stand about . . . could have;* should these verbs be rendered by the subjunctive in accordance with REF. 6, LN. XIV.?

⁵ *the more numerous . . . sent;* translate as if it read, *the more numerous letters and messengers were sent to Caesar.*

⁶ *than part;* **quam pars** is preferable to **parte** as it avoids a succession of ablatives.

⁷ *have . . . fame;* **sit** with Ablative of Quality.

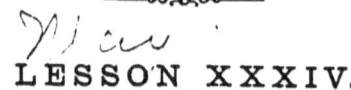

LESSON XXXIV.

THE ABLATIVE (*Continued*).

REFERENCES.

1-5. Of Price. A. & G. 252, *a–d:* A. & S. 252: B. 258 *c:* B. & M. 884: G. 404: H. 422, NOTES 1, 2.

6, 7. Of Specification. A. & G. 253: A. & S. 250: B. 261, RULE XLVI.: B. & M. 889: G. 398: H. 424, NOTE 1.

8-10. Of Time. A. & G. 256: A. & S. 253: B. 252, RULE XXVIII.: B. & M. 949: G. 392: H. 429.

11-16. *Ablative Absolute.* A. & G. 255, *a*, NOTE: A. & S. 257, REM. 1–5, 7: B. 264, RULE XLIX., *a–c:* B. & M. 965-967: G. 408; 409, REM. 1–3: H. 431, 1–4.

EXAMPLES.

1. This man sold his country for gold, **vendĭdit hic auro patriam.**

2. He sold an oration for twenty talents, **viginti talentis oratiōnem vendĭdit.**

3. He hired a house at no great price, **conduxit non magno domum.**

4. No curse has cost the human race more than anger, **nulla pestis humāno genĕri pluris stetit irā.**

5. The judges do not care a straw for the state, **judĭces rem publĭcam flocci non faciunt.**

6. Asia surpasses all lands in fruitfulness, **Asia ubertāte omnĭbus terris antecellit.**

7. A town, Bibrax by name, was eight miles distant, **oppĭdum, nomĭne Bibrax, abĕrat milia passuum octo.**
8. What did you do last night? **quid proxĭma nocte egisti?**
9. You were at the house of Lacca that night, **fuisti apud Laecam illa nocte.**
10. You will hear within three days, **triduo audiētis.**
11. Do you hesitate to do that when I order it, *or* at my bidding? **num dubĭtas id imperante me facĕre?**
12. Since no one hinders we shall carry on war, **nullo impediente bellum gerēmus.**
13. By destroying him danger is averted, **illo sublāto depellĭtur pericŭlum.**
14. In the consulship of Lepidus and Tullus, **Lepĭdo et Tullo consulĭbus.**
15. Which have been managed in his absence, **quae illo absente gesta sunt.**
16. Without stirring up any public commotion, **nullo tumultu publĭce concitāto.**

VOCABULARY 34.

commotion, **tumultus, us,** *m.*
conspiracy, **conjuratio, ōnis,** *f.*
cost, **sto, stare, steti, statum.**
enter upon, **ingredior, ingrĕdi, ingressus sum;** *w.* **in** *and acc.*
fruitfulness, productiveness, **ubertas, ātis,** *f.*
hire, **condūco, ĕre, duxi, ductum.**
justice, **aequĭtas, ātis,** *f.*

mercy, **misericordia, ae,** *f.*
name, **nomen, ĭnis,** *n.*
publicly, **pub!ĭce,** *adv.*
sell, **vendo, ĕre, vendĭdi, vendĭtum.**
sesterce, **sestertius, i,** *m.*: *a silver coin worth nearly four cents.*
stir up, **concĭto, āre, āvi, ātum.**
variety, **variĕtas, ātis,** *f.*

EXERCISE 34.

1. My brother's son fears that he shall not be able to sell his house for twenty thousand sesterces. 2. Last year we could have hired a house in this city for five thousand sesterces. 3. Although the Romans conquered the Gauls in many battles,[1] nevertheless the victories cost them much blood. 4. This general does not seem to care a straw for the lives of his soldiers. 5. He said that Asia was so fertile

and fruitful that it surpassed all lands² both in the productiveness of its fields and variety of its fruits. 6. We think that a city, Marseilles by name, is about ten miles distant. 7. There is no doubt that you surpassed yourself yesterday in justice and mercy. 8. I can not but think that he has entered upon this war under the guidance of the immortal gods. 9. It happened that in the consulship of Cicero many wretches formed³ a conspiracy against the republic. 10. I shall attempt to make him resign⁴ his praetorship without stirring up any public commotion. 11. Since the enemy did not hinder, we marched through their territory. 12. Within ten days you will hear that he inflicted severe punishment upon his slaves because his wife had been murdered. 13. The state will be freed from great danger by killing this man. 14. I asked the defendant why he was at the house of Marcellus last night⁵ and what he had done the night before. 15. He came in my absence to hire⁶ my house.

Notes and Questions.

[1] *in many battles;* see Ln. XXXII., Ref. 4, 5.
[2] *lands;* see Ln. XXVI., Ref. 1-7.
[3] *formed;* see Ln. IX., Ref. 4-8.
[4] *resign;* see Ln. IX., Ex. 6.
[5] *night;* put the word *night* in the second clause only.
[6] *to hire;* what does this infinitive denote?

LESSON XXXV.

EXPRESSIONS OF TIME.

REFERENCES.

1-3. *Time When or Within Which.* A. & G. 256; 259, *a, c:* A. & S. 253, Note 1: B. 251; 252: B. & M. 949; 951: G. 392; H. 429.

LATIN PROSE COMPOSITION.

4, 5. *Time How Long or During Which.* A. & G. 256; 259 c: A. & S. 236, Note 3: B. 220, Rule XI.: B. & M. 950; 951: G. 337; 338: H. 379.

6-8. *Use of Prepositions in Expressions of Time.* A. & G. 256 a; 259 b: A. & S. 236 Rem. 5: B. 252 Rem. 1; 220 Rem. 1: B. & M. 953: G. 337 Remark; 393, Remark: H. 379 1; 429 1, 2.

9-12. *Time Before or After an Event.* A. & G. 259 d: A. & S. 253 Rem. 1, (a.), (b.), Rem. 2: B. 252 Rem. 2: B. & M. 954; 957: G. 400 Rem. 3: H. 430, Note 1, 1)–3), Note 3.

EXAMPLES.

1. He finished the war in the middle of summer, **bellum media aestāte confēcit.**
2. You will hear within three days, **triduo audiētis.**
3. You wished to kill me at the last consular election, **proxĭmis comitiis consularībus me interficĕre voluisti.**
4. He has had a residence at Rome many years, **domicilium Romae multos annos habuit.**
5. He has reigned twenty-three years, **annum tertium et vicesĭmum regnat.**
6. Throughout these years, **per hosce annos.**
7. Caesar ordered the gates to be shut towards evening, **sub vespĕrum Caesar portas claudi jussit.**
8. It cannot be suppressed for all time, **non in perpetuum comprĭmi potest.**
9. A few days afterwards the senate was freed from danger, **liberātus pericŭlo paucis post diēbus senātus.**
10. The act was performed three days afterwards, **post diem tertium gesta res est.**
11. An envoy had been killed a few years before, **paucis ante annis legātus interfectus erat.**
12. You were quaestor fourteen years ago, **quaestor fuisti abhinc annos quattuordĕcim.**
13. On the 31st of Oct., in the consulship of Lepidus and Tullus, **pridie Kalendas Novembres, Lepĭdo et Tullo consulibus;** *which may be abbreviated to,* **prid. Kal. Nov. Lepĭdo et Tullo coss.**
14. On the first of June all was changed, **Kalendis Juniis mutāta omnia.**

15. For the 28th of Oct., **in ante diem quintum Kalendas Novembres;** *or*, **in a. d. v. Kal. Nov.**

VOCABULARY 35.

check, restrain, hinder, **reprĭmo, ĕre, pressi, pressum.**
decree, **decerno, ĕre, crēvi, crētum.**
evening, towards evening, **sub vespĕrum.**
finish, **conficio, ficĕre, fēci, fectum.**
following, **postĕrus, a, um.**
light, daylight, **lux, lucis,** *f.;* a little before daylight, **paulo ante lucem.**
memory, within the memory of man, **post homĭnum memoriam.**

midnight, a little after midnight, **paulo post mediam noctem.**
perhaps, **fortasse,** *adv.*
short, **brevis, e.**
suppress, **comprĭmo, ĕre, pressi, pressum.**
thanksgiving, **supplicatio, ōnis,** *f.*
time, for all time, **in perpetuum,** *sc.* **tempus.**
while, for a little while, **paulisper,** *adv.*
yesterday, day before yesterday, **nudius tertius.**

EXERCISE 35.

1. If you had carried on the war more vigorously, you would have finished it in the last part of winter. 2. Who can be so stupid as to think[1] that the Gauls will come within five days to attack us? 3. I heard day before yesterday that you wished to kill me at the last consular election. 4. Men came on the following day that they might urge[2] us to march[3] either towards evening or a little after midnight. 5. If Catiline alone should be killed,[4] the conspiracy would perhaps be checked for a little while, but it would not be suppressed for all time. 6. He says that this king, who has already reigned twenty-four years,[5] is much younger than his brother. 7. He has lived many years in this city and throughout these years no one has been angry with him.[6] 8. If this has happened to no one within the memory of man, will you not go into exile? 9. There is no doubt that men can be found who will

relieve you of this care and promise to kill[7] me in my bed on that very night, a little before daylight. ✓10. We can not but think that you could have finished the war many years before. 11. Because so many nations surrendered to him within so short a time, a thanksgiving was decreed for the twenty-sixth of December.[8] 12. This wretch promised that for three thousand sesterces[9] he would kill you on the twenty-fifth of October. ✓13. Five days afterwards he would have been condemned for treason, if we had not protected him. 14. We had a long controversy with these men three days ago. 15. Would that I could have been present on the first of August![10]

Notes and Questions.

[1] *as to think;* see LN. IX., REF. 1–3.
[2] *that they might urge;* see LN. VII., REF. 12, 13.
[3] *to march;* see LN. VIII., REF. 1–14.
[4] *If . . . killed;* in what two ways may this be expressed? See LN. XI., REF. 1–15, and LN. XXXIV., REF. 11–16.
[5] *has reigned . . . years;* see Ex. 5.
[6] *angry with him;* see LN. XXV., REF. 6–11.
[7] *to kill;* verbs signifying *hope, promise, undertake,* are followed by the accusative of the personal pronoun and the future infinitive.
[8] *for the twenty-sixth of December;* for determining how to write this and similar dates, see A. & G. 259 *c;* 376, *a–d;* A. & S. 326, (1)–(12): B. 374, *a–c:* B. & M. 1524–1537: G. *page* 387: H. 641–645.
[9] *for three thousand sesterces;* see LN. XXXIV., REF. 1–5.
[10] *of August;* **sextilis, e.**

LESSON XXXVI.

PLACE.

REFERENCES.

1, 2. *Place from which.* A. & G. 258, *a:* A. & S. 255: B. 254, RULE XXXIX.: B. & M. 911: G. 411: H. 412, I., II.

3, 4. *Place to which.* A. & G. 258, *b;* A. & S. 237: B. 221, Rule XII.: B. & M. 938: G. 410: H. 380, I., II.

5-7. *Place at or in which.* A. & G. 258 *c;* A. & S. 221: 254: B. 249, Rule XXVII., Note: B. & M. 932-934: G. 412: H. 425, I., II., 2.

8-10. *Place by, through, or over which.* A. & G. 258 *g;* A. & S. 255 2: B. 258 *e;* B. & M. 941; 942: G. 387: H. 420, 3).

2, 4, 7. *Words used like Names of Towns.* A. & G. 258 *c* Remark, *d;* A. & S. 221 Rem. 1, 3; 237 Rem. 4: B. 221; 254 Rem. 1: B. & M. 943; 944: G. 410, Rem. 1, 2; 411; 412 Rem. 1: H. 412 1; 380 2, 1); 426, 2.

11, 12. *Ablative of Place at, in, or on which.* A. & G. 258 *f:* A. & S. 254 Rem. 1-3: B. 253: B. & M. 937, 1-3; 947: G. 384-387: H. 425 2.

13-16. *How to express towards a Place, etc.* A. & G. 258 *f* Remark; 259 *f, g;* A. & S. 232 Rem. 2: B. 221 Rem. 1; 254 Rem. 2: G. 410 Rem. 3-5: H. 380 1; 412 3, Note.

EXAMPLES.

1. He set out from Rome, **Romā profectus est.**
2. He set out from home, **domo profectus est.**
3. He will betake himself to Marseilles, **se Massiliam confĕret.**
4. Men go into the country, **rus homĭnes eunt.**
5. He had a residence in Rome, **domicilium Romae habuit.**
6. Themistocles, a very eminent man at Athens, said, **Themistocles, summus Athēnis vir, dixit.**
7. Consultations which he had at home, **deliberatiōnes quas habēbat domi.**
8. We shall march through Athens, **iter per Athēnas faciēmus.**
9. He set out by the Aurelian way, **Aurelia via profectus est.**
10. The corn, which he had brought up the river Arar, **frumento, quod flumĭne Arăre subvexĕrat.**
11. All things have been brought into a state of peace on land and sea, **omnia sunt terra marīque pacāta.**
12. What poisoner in all Italy? **quis tota Italia venefĭcus?**
13. Towards Rome, in *or* into the vicinity of Rome, **ad Romam.**
14. Near Rome, **ad Romam, apud Romam.**
15. From Rome, from near Rome, **a Roma.**
16. From Rome, out of Rome, **e Roma.**

VOCABULARY 36.

annex, join to, **adjungo, ĕre, junxi, junctum.**
carry up, **subveho, ĕre, vexi, vectum.**
difficult, **difficĭlis, e.**
field, in the field, **militiae.**
middle, **medius, a, um.**
nearly, **paene,** *adv.*
perform, **gero, ĕre, gessi, gestum.**

safe, **tutus, a, um.**
sea, **mare, maris,** *n.*
set out, **proficiscor, i, profectus sum.**
still, even now, **etiam nunc,** *adv.*
strong, firm, **firmus, a, um.**
summon, **voco, āre, āvi, ātum.**
vicissitude, **variĕtas, ātis,** *f.*
way, road, **via, ae,** *f.*

EXERCISE 36.

1. Cicero said that Pompey, within forty-nine days[1] after he had set out from Brundisium, annexed the whole of Cilicia to the government[2] of the Roman people. 2. He asked whether the consul had already gone from home or[3] was still at Geneva. 3. We answered that he had set out for Athens five days before. 4. Since we had already had a residence at Marseilles for many years, we set out from that city and came to Rome. 5. The orator asked the senate what place on the whole sea had had so strong a garrison throughout those years that it was safe. 6. He says that yesterday, when he had been nearly killed at his own home, he summoned the senate into the temple of Jupiter Stator. 7. This envoy has come to tell how great deeds our general has performed[4] at home and in the field, on land and sea. 8. He says that this war, although it is great and difficult and has been carried on with[5] much vicissitude on land and sea, will be wholly finished[6] by this man in the middle of summer. 9. If we had set out from Rome ten days ago, we should have gone by the Appian way. 10. We ought to have used the corn, which we had carried up the river Rhine in our ships.[7] 11. In the consulship of Metellus we lived in the country, but five years afterwards we came to the town of Brundisium.

12. This man came from near Rome and has now set out towards Naples. 13. Let us stay in the vicinity of this city until our friends arrive.[8] 14. Let us go into the country before our friends come[9] to visit us. 15. What man in all America is so cowardly as not to be willing to die for[10] his country?

Notes and Questions.

[1] *within forty-nine days;* render as if it read, *on the forty-ninth day.*
[2] *to the government;* repeat the preposition **ad.**
[3] *or;* how should it be rendered in a double question?
[4] *has performed;* see LN. XVI., REF. 9–14.
[5] *with;* render with **in.**
[6] *will be finished;* see LN. XXIV., NOTE 4.
[7] *in our ships;* see LN. XXXII., REF. 4, 5.
[8] *until . . . arrive;* see LN. XV., REF. 8–10.
[9] *before . . . come;* see LN. XV., REF. 3, 4.
[10] *for;* how should it be translated? See LN. XXV., REF. 14, 15.

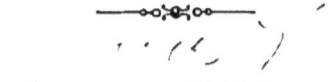

LESSON XXXVII.

USE OF PARTICIPLES.

REFERENCES.

1-10. *Tenses.* A. & G. 290, *b, d:* A. & S. 274, 2: B. 323, RULE LXXV.; B. & M. 1343: G. 278; 279: H. 550.

1-10. *Different Uses.* A. & G. 289; 291, *a, b;* 292, *a:* 293 *a, c:* A. & S. 274 REM. 3, 5, 6, 7, 8; 274 3 (*a.*): B. 318–323: B. & M. 1348–1354: G. 438; 439; 536; 537: H. 548; 549, 1–5, NOTES 1, 2.

EXAMPLES.

1. I summoned to my presence Gabinius, (who was) surmising nothing as yet, **Gabinium ad me, nihil dum suspicantem, vocāvi.**

2. Shall we put up with Catiline, (who is) longing to lay waste the earth? **Catilīnam, orbem terrae vastāre cupientem, perferēmus?**

3. His arrival kept back Mithridates (who had been) puffed up by an unusual victory, **hujus adventus Mithridātem insolīta inflātum victoria continuit.**

4. Who saved this same city (after it was) founded and enlarged, **qui eandem hanc urbem condĭtam amplificatamque servāvit.**

5. Having laid waste the fields and set fire to the villages they hastened towards Caesar's camp, **agros depopulāti, vicis incensis, ad castra Caesăris contendērunt.**

6. After roaming about they came through to the Rhine, **vagāti ad Rhenum pervenērunt.**

7. I crossed the Rhine because I had been invited by the Gauls, **transii Rhenum arcessītus a Gallis.**

8. He assigned to Cassius the city to be set on fire, **attribuit urbem inflammandam [8] Cassio.**

9. Pray what would have been the result if (the shops) had been burned? **quid tandem (tabernis) incensis futūrum fuit?**

10. After, *or* since, the founding of the city, **post urbem condĭtam.**

VOCABULARY 37.

alarm, **commoveo, ēre, mōvi, mōtum.**
attack, **aggredior, aggrĕdi, aggressus sum.**
cut down, **occīdo, ĕre, cīdi, cīsum.**
earth, **orbis terrārum** *or* **terrae; orbis, is,** *m.*
hither, **citerior, citerius.**
invite, send for, **arcesso, ĕre, arcessīvi, arcessītum.**
keep back, restrain, **contineo, ēre, tinui, tentum.**
lay waste, **vasto, āre, āvi, ātum.**

learn, **cognosco, ĕre, cognōvi, cognĭtum.**
long, long for, desire eagerly, **cupio, cupĕre, cupīvi** *or* **cupii, cupĭtum.**
new, **novus, a, um.**
put up with, bear with, endure, **perfĕro, perferre, pertŭli, perlātum.**
set fire to, burn, **incendo, ĕre, incendi, incensum.**
sight, **conspectus, us,** *m.*
take away, **removeo, ēre, mōvi, mōtum.**

EXERCISE 37.

1. Ought we, the consuls, to put up with these men, who are longing to lay waste the whole earth? 2. After setting fire to many villages[1] they hastened towards Rome

by the Appian way. 3. The king said that he crossed the Rhine because he had been invited by the Gauls. 4. Caesar, having been alarmed by these letters, enlisted two new legions in hither Gaul. 5. He summoned to his presence[2] the generals who knew nothing as yet[3] with respect to the affair. 6. The general kept back his soldiers in camp who had been greatly alarmed by the arrival of the enemy. 7. He assigned to Catiline all the citizens to be robbed and butchered. 8. Pray, what would you have done if all the villages had been burned?[4] 9. The lieutenant, after taking away the horses out of sight and exhorting the cavalry to fight bravely, began the battle on the left wing. 10. The consul ordered his troops after they had been led[5] out of camp to wheel about and advance to the attack. 11. The enemy having attacked our army on the march, cut down a large number of the infantry. 12. Since the founding of the city this is the only case that has been met with[6] in which all patriotic citizens agreed.[7] 13. After learning these facts we hastened into the vicinity of Marseilles. 14. Although I have been invited I shall not cross the Rhine. 15. Since the consul has learned these facts, he will invite the conspirators into the country and set fire to all their houses.

Notes and Questions.

[1] *after setting fire to villages;* Latin verbs, except deponents, have no perfect active participle; hence the necessity for the ablative absolute which is used to supply this want.

[2] *to his presence;* see Ex. 1.   [3] *nothing as yet;* **nihil dum.**

[4] *if . . . burned;* render by the ablative absolute.

[5] *after they had been led;* translate as if it read, *having been led.*

[6] *this . . . met with;* translate as if it read, *this case alone has been met*

[7] *agreed;* see LN. X., REF. 1-9.

[8] See Gildersleeve, 279 REM.; 431.

LESSON XXXVIII.

THE GERUND AND GERUNDIVE.

REFERENCES.

1 - 8. A. & G. 295-298, *a:* A. & S. 275, I., II., III. Rem. 1, (4):
B. 324, *a, c,* 1, 2; 325, Rule LXXVI.: B. & M. 1304; 1319-1322;
1327; 1330: G. 426-429, Rem. 1: H. 541; 542, I., Note 1; 543.

EXAMPLES.

1. Practice in speaking, **dicendi exercitatio.**
2. Night made an end of besieging, **finem oppugnandi nox fecit.**
3. Opportunity for hurling javelins, **spatium pila conjiciendi.**
4. They went out for the purpose of plundering, **praedandi causa egressi sunt.**
5. He gave the signal for beginning battle, **proeli committendi signum dedit.**
6. For the purpose of killing the consuls, **consŭlum interficiendōrum causa.**
7. This most strongly fortified place for holding the senate, **hic munitissĭmus habendi senātus locus.**
8. For the purpose of saving themselves, **sui conservandi causa.**

VOCABULARY 38.

besiege, **oppugno, āre, āvi, ātum.**
encourage, **consōlor, āri, ātus sum.**
give up, abandon, **abjicio, jicĕre, jēci, jectum.**
keep, **asservo, āre, āvi, ātum.**
leading men, chief men, **princĭpes, um,** *m. pl.*
lessen, **levo, āre, āvi, ātum.**
threats, **minae, ārum,** *f. pl.*

observe, **cognosco, ĕre, cognōvi, cognĭtum.**
practice, **exercitatio, ōnis,** *f.*
prepare, **paro, āre, āvi, ātum.**
privilege, power, **potestas, ātis,** *f.*
save, **conservo, āre, āvi, ātum.**
style, **genus, ĕris,** *n.*
suffer, permit, **patior, pati, passus sum.**
unusual, **insitātus, a, um.**
violence, **vis, vis,** *f.*

EXERCISE 38.

1. After encouraging the defendant, I asked him to make an end of entreating. 2. The orator asked the judges to suffer[1] him to make[1] use of an unusual style of speaking. 3. Have you not often observed how great[2] influence this orator exerts[3] from this very place by reason of copiousness in speaking? 4. Would that I had[4] the privilege of coming into this place! 5. If this wretch should give up his plan of making war, it would be said[5] that he had been driven out into exile with violence and threats. 6. For the purpose of avoiding suspicion you dared to ask[6] the consul to keep[6] you at his home. 7. Never, fellow-citizens, for the purpose of lessening my unpopularity, have I asked you not to lay violent hands upon these conspirators. 8. I asked whether citizens were fleeing from Rome for the purpose of saving themselves or of checking your designs. 9. Let him, if he wishes, make use of arms for the purpose of defending himself. 10. Give the signal for beginning battle, if you wish us to advance to the attack. 11. We fear that this man will prepare a band for the purpose of killing the consuls and leading men of the state. 12. There is no doubt that this orator has had great practice in speaking. 13. If you had had greater practice in fighting, you would not have fled for the purpose of saving yourself. 14. When night had made an end of besieging, a man of very great influence[7] among his friends came to beg for peace. 15. Who is so stupid as to think that citizens have fled from the city for the purpose of saving themselves?

Notes and Questions.

[1] *to suffer* . . . *to make ;* should each of these infinitives be rendered with an infinitive?

[2] *how great;* **quantum;** see LN. XXX., REF. 1-6.

[3] *exert influence ;* **valeo, ēre ui, itum ;** what mood must be used?

LATIN PROSE COMPOSITION.   103

⁴ *Would that I had;* see Ln. XXVI., Ref. 8-11, and Ln. V., Ref. 8-9.
⁵ *it would be said;* see Ln. XXIII., Note 5.
⁶ *to ask . . . to keep;* see Note 1.
⁷ *of very great influence;* see Ln. XXXIII., Ref. 10, 11.

———oo≈o≈oo———

LESSON XXXIX.

THE GERUND AND GERUNDIVE (*Continued*).

REFERENCES.

1-9. A. & G. 299-301; 294 *d:* A. & S. 275 III. Rem. 2, 3, 4: B. 324, *b, d, e;* 325, Rule LXXVI.: B. & M. 1332; 1337; 1338; 1340: G. 430-434: H. 542, II., III., Note 2, IV.; 544, 1, 2, Notes 1, 2.

EXAMPLES.

1. The consul gives attention to appeasing the gods, **consul placandis dis dat opĕram.**
2. For making a camp, **ad castra facienda.**
3. One of whom could furnish subjects for writing, **quorum alter res ad scribendum adhibēre potĕrat.**
4. He invited Gauls for the purpose of overturning the foundations of our government, **ad evertenda fundamenta rei publicae Gallos arcessit.**
5. He assigned to Cassius the city to be set on fire, *or* the firing of the city, **attribuit urbem inflammandam Cassio.**
6. They have strengthened the conspiracy by not believing, **conjuratiōnem non credendo corroborāvērunt.**
7. By badly managing their business, **male gerendo negotio.**
8. In punishing Lentulus, **in Lentŭlo puniendo.**
9. With respect to choosing a commander, **de imperatōre deligendo.**

VOCABULARY 39

choose, **delīgo, ĕre, lēgi, lectum.**
confer, consign, **mando, āre, āvi, ātum.**
debt, **aes aliēnum, aeris aliēni,** *n.*
desire, **voluntas, ātis,** *f.*
draw, portray, **exprĭmo, ĕre, pressi, pressum.**

fall into, **incĭdo, ĕre, incĭdi, incāsum.**
historian, **rerum auctor, rerum scriptor.**
invested, **occupātus, a, um.**
lie in wait, **insidior, āri, ātus sum.**
look at, **intueor, ēri, tuĭtus sum.**
maintain, **retineo, ēre, tinui, tentum.**
manage, **gero, ĕre, gessi, gestum.**
portraiture, **imāgo, ĭnis,** *f.*
provoke, **lacesso, ĕre, ĭvi** *or* **ii** *or* **i, ītum.**
revenue, **vectīgal, ālis,** *n.*
silent, keep silent, **taceo, ēre, ui, ĭtum.**
strengthen, **corrobŏro, āre, āvi, ātum.**
stake, is at stake, **agĭtur.**
torch, **fax, facis,** *f.*

EXERCISE 39.

1. You ought to give attention to tilling your fields. 2. He sent men to promise[1] a large number of ships for transporting the army. 3. This king having been provoked thought that an opportunity was offered him[2] for taking our city. 4. I fear that they will not cease[3] to lie in wait for the consul at his own home and to prepare torches for firing the city. 5. How many portraitures of distinguished men, drawn not only to be looked at[4] but also to be imitated,[4] do you think historians have left us?[5] 6. We could have overcome[6] you, not by fighting but by keeping silent. 7. You ought not to strengthen this conspiracy by not believing. 8. It remains for me to speak[7] briefly with respect to choosing a commander. 9. I have[8] as much influence[9] as you have given me by conferring honors. 10. The orator said that he had as much capability as an almost daily practice in speaking had been able to bring him. 11. Our property is at stake, invested in farming your revenues. 12. By badly managing their business these men have fallen into great debt. 13. There is no one who thinks[10] that there can be any cruelty in punishing the consul.

Notes and Questions.

[1] *to promise;* see Ln. VII., Ref. 12, 13.
[2] *him;* see Ln. III., Ref. 8-12, and Ln. XXVI., Ref. 1-7.
[3] *will not cease;* see Ln. VIII., Note 8.
[4] *to be looked at . . . to be imitated*; render with **ad** and the Gerundive.
[5] *us;* see Ln. XXV., Ref. 1-3.
[6] *we could have overcome;* see Ln. XVII., Ex. 13.
[7] *for me to speak;* see Ln. IX., Ref. 4-8.
[8] *I have,* etc. When the thing possessed is a quality of the possessor, the possessor is usually put in the ablative with **in**, and the thing possessed in the nominative with **est**: e. g. *I have wisdom,* **in me est sapientia**; *I have as much natural ability, as* etc., **ingeni in me tantum est, quantum** etc.
[9] *influence;* see Ln. XXII., Ref. 6-8.
[10] *who thinks;* see Ln. X., Ref. 1-9.

LESSON XL.

THE PERIPHRASTIC CONJUGATIONS. — THE SUPINE.

REFERENCES.

1-3. *First Periphrastic Conjugation.* A. & G. 129; 293 *a, c:* A. & S. 162 14: B. 94, *a:* B. & M. 328: G. 149; 238; 239: H. 233.

4-9. *Second Periphrastic Conjugation.* A. & G. 129; 294, *b, c:* A. & S. 162 15; 274 Rem. 8, 11: B. 94, *b:* B. & M. 329; 1305: G. 150; 243: H. 234; 466 Note.

5, 7. *Dative of Agent.* A. & G. 232: A. & S. 225 III.: B. 248 Rule XXXVI.: B. & M. 847: G. 353: H. 388.

10, 11. *Supine in* um. A. & G. 302, Remark: A. & S. 276, I., II.: B. 326, Rule LXXVII.: B. & M. 1360: G. 435; 436: H. 545, Notes 1, 2; 546, 1-4.

12. *Supine in* u. A. & G. 303: A. & S. 276 III.: B. 326, Rule LXXVIII.: B. & M. 1365: G. 437, Rem. 1: H. 547, 1, 2.

EXAMPLES.

1. I am, was, *etc.* about to go,
I am, was, *etc.* likely to go,
I am, was, *etc.* going to go, } **ego sum, eram,** *etc.* **itūrus.**
I am, was, *etc.* intending to go,
I am, was, *etc.* to go,

2. They seem to me more likely to make vows against the republic than to bear arms, **magis mihi videntur vota factūri contra rem publĭcam quam arma latūri.**

3. What would have been the result if the shops had been burned? **quid tabernis incensis futūrum fuit?**

4. A proper limit in speaking must be sought, **modus in dicendo quaerendus est.**

5. We must contend with extravagance, **cum luxuria nobis certandum est.**

6. Whatever will need to be cut off, *or* whatever will have to be cut off, I shall not suffer to remain, **quae resecanda erunt, non patiar manēre.**

7. I did not need to fear, **verendum mihi non erat.**

8. The highest welfare must not be too often endangered, **non est saepius summa salus periclitanda.**

9. If he were a private citizen, he ought to be chosen, **si privātus esset, erat deligendus.**

10. I shut out those, whom you had sent to me to pay their respects, **exclūsi eos, quos tu ad me salutātum misĕras.**

11. He came to Rome to demand aid, **Romam venit auxilium postulātum.**

12. It is difficult to say how much we are hated, **difficĭle est dictu quanto in odio simus.**

VOCABULARY 40.

address, **allŏquor, i, locūtus sum.**
ask for, demand, **postŭlo, āre, āvi, ātum.**
assassin, murderer, **sicarius, i,** *m.*
complain, **queror, i, questus sum.**
decide, **judĭco, āre, āvi, ātum.**
defend, **defendo, ĕre, fendi, fensum.**
disaster, **calamĭtas, ātis,** *f.*
hated, to be hated, **in odio esse,** *w. dat. of person by whom hated.*
now, **nunc, jam,** *adv.*
neighbors, **finitĭmi, ōrum,** *m. pl.*
pay one's respects, **salūto, āre, āvi, ātum.**
safe, **salvus, a, um.**

spirit, **anĭmus, i,** *m.*
to-day, **hodiernus dies, hodierni diēi,** *m.*

very difficult, **perdifficĭlis, e.**

EXERCISE 40.

1. Believe me,[1] fellow-citizens, this assassin is not intending to go into exile. 2. These men seem to us more likely to withdraw from allegiance to the republic than to carry on war with her enemies. 3. These assassins must be driven out into exile if we wish[2] the city to be safe. 4. We must either live with our fellow-citizens or die for them.[3] 5. You must defend this city not only from[4] disaster but also from[4] the fear of disaster. 6. The senators must decide to-day with respect to their own lives[5] and the lives[5] of their wives and children. 7. We did not need to fear that our enemies would not give up their plan of making war. 8. In what spirit[6] ought you to bear this, that citizens have fled[7] from Rome for the purpose of saving themselves. 9. If we wish to be good citizens, we must defend the name and welfare of the state. 10. We ought to thank the immortal gods because we have won so great a victory. 11. Many came to me on that day[8] to pay their respects and to complain[9] because the consul had dissolved[10] the senate. 12. I must address my fellow-citizens with respect to the election of consuls.[11] 13. It is very difficult to say how much you are hated by all your neighbors. 14. If this were the best thing to do, I should not suffer you to live a moment of time.

Notes and Questions.

[1] *me ;* see L.N. XXV., Ref. 6-11.

[2] *if we wish,* etc. ; what kind of a supposition is expressed by this sentence ?

[3] *for them ;* see L.N. XXV., Ref. 14, 15.

[4] *from ;* a.   [5] *lives ;* see L.N. XXI., Note 1.

[6] *In what spirit ;* see L.N. XXXII., Ref. 1.

⁷ *that citizens have fled ;* render with accusative and infinitive, appositive with **hoc.**

⁸ *on that day ;* what time is denoted by the ablative ? What by the accusative ?

⁹ *to pay their respects and to complain ;* see EXAMPLES 10 and 11.

¹⁰ *had dissolved ;* which mood is preferable ? See LN. XIV., REF. 1-5 and NOTE 5.

¹¹ *with respect to the election of consuls ;* translate as if it read, *with respect to electing consuls.*

EXERCISES FOR GENERAL REVIEW AND EXAMINATION.

The following Exercises are intended for oral recitation, without any previous preparation. They contain only such words as have been given in the preceding Vocabularies, and illustrate only such principles as have been illustrated in the preceding Lessons. I. - IV. is not to be recited till after Lesson IV. has been learned; V. - VIII., till after Lesson VIII., and so on to the end. The design is to put the same principle in many different ways, so as to enable the teacher to ascertain whether the scholar fully comprehends it; whether he has made it a part of himself; this aids in securing thoroughness and also adds life and interest to the study. Probably, time will not permit all the sentences to be given; on the other hand, the teacher may find it profitable to form others; it will be seen that they may be multiplied almost indefinitely.

I-IV.

1. Who of us will be elected consul? 2. You and I have not been elected consuls. 3. Neither you nor I had been elected consul. 4. Who was the first to reach the top of the hill? 5. We were the first to reach the top of the hill. 6. You will be the first to reach the top of the hill. 7. Our soldiers had been the first to reach the top of the hill. 8. This man was the first who betook himself into the middle of the city. 9. The man and woman whom you saw will betake themselves into the middle of the city. 10. This consul will be the first to lead his soldiers into winter-quarters. 11. That consul was the first to lead his soldiers out of winter-quarters. 12. The enemy came in great numbers and made an attack upon us. 13. Our soldiers were very unwilling to make an attack upon them. 14. We hastened gladly to make an attack upon you.

15. Some of them were very unwilling to make an attack upon us. 16. One man came from one city, another from another. 17. Some of the enemy betook themselves in one direction, others in another. 18. Some led their troops in one direction, others in another. 19. The one party withdrew upon a mountain, the other betook themselves into the middle of the city. 20. They likewise betook themselves to their friends. 21. This man and woman gladly surrendered themselves and all their possessions to Caesar. 22. They will likewise surrender themselves and all their possessions to me. 23. Who of you will surrender himself and all his possessions to me? 24. I shall surrender myself and all my possessions to you. 25. These very men have surrendered themselves and all their possessions to him.

V.-VIII.

1. Break up camp as soon as possible. 2. Do not hesitate to break up camp as soon as possible. 3. Let us break up camp as soon as possible. 4. Would that you had not broken up camp! 5. O that we were breaking up camp! 6. May you not break up camp! 7. He has been delaying now a long time in the vicinity of this city. 8. He had been delaying a long time in the vicinity of this city. 9. While he was delaying in the vicinity of this city, I was marching. 10. If he delays for the sake of supplies, I shall not march. 11. We delayed so as to avoid the suspicion of fear. 12. The soldiers had delayed that they might avoid the suspicion of fear. 13. These men have delayed that they may avoid the suspicion of fear. 14. We shall delay in order to avoid the suspicion of fear. 15. Let us delay that we may avoid the suspicion of fear. 16. We shall employ the Gauls to terrify the

enemy. 17. We employed the Gauls to terrify these soldiers. 18. They had employed us to terrify you. 19. You will send forward men to terrify the enemy. 20. The consul sent forward soldiers to make an attack upon the enemy. 21. We fear that they will not advance to the attack. 22. Do not fear that they will not advance to the attack. 23. You fear that they will wheel about. 24. Who feared that the enemy would wheel about. 25. We ourselves had feared that they would wheel about and advance to the attack.

IX.-XII.

1. The general inflicts punishment upon his soldiers. 2. The general has inflicted punishment upon his soldiers. 3. The general will inflict punishment upon his soldiers. 4. The soldiers are so wicked that their general will inflict punishment upon them. 5. The soldiers were so wicked that their general inflicted very severe punishment upon them. 6. We fear that these soldiers are so wicked that their general will inflict most severe punishment upon them. 7. We fear that these soldiers are so wicked that we shall not be able to hinder their general from inflicting most severe punishment upon them. 8. There is not even a doubt that these soldiers are so wicked as to fear that they will not be able to hinder their general from inflicting most severe punishment upon them. 9. We made them defend our city. 10. It happened that they were defending the city. 11. These soldiers are not suitable to defend our city. 12. There were some who did not defend their city. 13. Our soldiers could not be restrained from defending their city. 14. If Caius stays, he will pay his tax. 15. Provided Caius stays in the city, he will pay his tax. 16. If Caius should stay, he would

pay his tax. 17. If Caius had staid, he would have paid his tax. 18. If Caius were staying in the city, he would pay his tax. 19. There is not even a doubt that if Caius stays in this city, some one will prevent him from paying his tax. 20. Provided he does not inform me with respect to your arrival, I shall inflict punnishment upon him. 21. But if he should inform me with respect to your arrival, I should not inflict punishment upon him. 22. We shuddered at his cruelty as if he were present. 23. Do not shudder at his cruelty as if he were present. 24. Let us not shudder at the cruelty of the absent Caius as if he were present. 25. We shall not shudder at his cruelty as if he were present.

XIII.-XVI.

1. Although we fought till late at night, we routed no one. 2. Although they had fought till late at night, they were not conquered. 3. We did not complain, although we were thrown into great disorder. 4. Although we could not get a firm footing, still we kept in line. 5. We were thrown into great disorder because we could not get a firm footing. 6. We shall be thrown into great disorder because we cannot get a firm footing. 7. We did not keep in line because we could not get a firm footing. 8. The French are complaining because the Germans have ravaged their country. 9. The Germans complained because the French had ravaged their country. 10. The Germans will complain because the French have renewed the war. 11. Let us not complain because we can not renew the war. 12. We shall return before you arrive. 13. After we arrived, you hastened to return. 14. Caius hastened to return as soon as you arrived. 15. When we arrived you hastened to return. 16. When Caesar arrives, his lieu-

tenant will return. 17. Wait until we arrive. 18. We shall wait until the soldiers come. 19. Who will wait until the general comes? I. 20. We are waiting to see whether he will come or not. 21. We did not march until the enemy recovered from fright. 22. Let us not march until the enemy recover from fright. 23. Let us make an attack before the enemy recovers from fright. 24. Will you go, or stay? I shall go. 25. Who would flee as a deserter? I would not.

XVII.-XX.

1. Caesar ought to make you this requital. 2. You must make Caesar this requital. 3. We may make them this requital. 4. These men can make you this requital. 5. They ought to have made us this requital. 6. He could have made you this requital. 7. I might have made him this requital. 8. He says that we ought not to give back the hostages. 9. He said that we ought not to give back the hostages. 10. He thinks that we can see the tower approaching. 11. He thought that we could see the tower approaching. 12. He thought that we could have seen the tower approaching. 13. He begs permission to give back the hostages. 14. We begged permission to give back the hostages. 15. Let us not beg permission to give back the hostages. 16. Do not beg permission to give back the hostages. 17. He declared that we ought not to have begged permission to give back the hostages. 18. We hear that the king is increasing his private property. 19. We hear that the king's private property is increasing. 20. We heard that the king was increasing his private property. 21. We heard that the king's private property was increasing. 22. The king said that he should increase his private property. 23. The king said that his

private property would increase. 24. Caesar says that if the Gauls give back the hostages, he will reward them. 25. He said that if the Gauls should give back the hostages, they would be rewarded. 26. He says that if the Gauls had given back the hostages, he would have rewarded them. 27. He said that if the Gauls had given back the hostages, they would have been rewarded. 28. He says that the men whom we saw on the top of the hill are soldiers. 29. He said that the men whom we saw on the top of the hill were soldiers. 30. Let us not forget that this is our country.

XXI.-XXIV.

1. We ought to care for the prosperity of our country. 2. It is wise to care for the prosperity of the country. 3. Let us not bring to destruction and desolation the houses of the city. 4. It is the duty of the general to care for the welfare of his soldiers. 5. It is your duty to care for the welfare of your army. 6. It is foolish to withdraw from allegiance to the state. 7. It is the part of wisdom to see that the welfare of the state cannot be separated from the welfare of the citizens. 8. Let us not endeavor to bring about the destruction of the commonwealth. 9. Do not endeavor to bring about the destruction of the commonwealth. 10. Pray, who would endeavor to bring about the destruction of the commonwealth? 11. I shall bestow upon you as much praise as is due a brave man. 12. He bestowed upon me as much praise as was due a brave man. 13. You said that you would bestow as much praise upon him as was due a great commander. 14. He feared that this city had not sufficient garrison. 15. We fear that this town has not sufficient garrison. 16. It is worth while for you to endure unpopularity. 17. There is no doubt that it is

worth while for me to endure unpopularity. 18. This man wishes to become participant in the public council. 19. Who would wish to become participant in this council? 20. No one has wished to become participant in this council. 21. I remember your kindness. 22. Do you remember his kindness? 23. I am not ashamed of you. 24. Are you ashamed of me? 25. This old man repents of his deeds. 26. You ought to repent of your inactivity and negligence. 27. This man is very skilful in military affairs and ought not to be condemned to death. 28. It is of great importance to Marcellus whether you repent of your deeds or not. 29. It is of great importance to me whether he comes or not. 30. It is of the highest importance to all that they have sound bodies and sound minds.

XXV.-XXVII.

1. If you consult me, I shall not be angry with you. 2. If you consult my interests, I shall not be angry with you. 3. If I ask your advice, will you be angry with me? 4. If he does not ask my advice, I shall not pardon him. 5. We seem to satisfy the republic, if we avoid the weapons of these men. 6. Will he lay violent hands upon me? 7. Did you think that he would lay violent hands upon me? 8. The senate would have laid violent hands upon me in this very place, if I had driven him out into exile. 9. If we go to meet them, they will lay violent hands upon us. 10. If we should go to meet them, they would lay violent hands upon us. 11. If you had gone to meet them, they would have laid violent hands upon you. 12. He said that if we should go to meet them, they would lay violent hands upon us. 13. We can not protect our city with this army. 14. What city have you protected with your cavalry? 15. You can not but protect us with

your infantry. 16. There is not even a doubt that you ought to protect us with your army. 17. We can not withstand them by our own efforts. 18. Who could have withstood you by his own efforts? 19. He ought to have withstood us by his own efforts. 20. You have me as a witness that you withstood him by your own efforts. 21. We have you as a witness that we withstood them by our own efforts. 22. There is no doubt but that his country is most dear to him. 23. I can not but think that you are like me. 24. He thinks that you are very unfriendly to him. 25. He asked me whether you were unfriendly to me. 26. We ought to be willing to die for our country. 27. Citizens ought to obey the decrees of the senate. 28. We, fellow-citizens, must obey the decrees of the senate. 29. It did not please them to obey the decrees of the senate. 30. Let us obey the decrees of the senate.

XXVIII.-XXX.

1. Do not grieve for my misfortune. 2. We can not but grieve for the misfortunes of the state. 3. Do not doubt that we shall win a great victory. 4. You will win a great victory, if you conquer this enemy. 5. If our general wins a victory, the senate will thank him. 6. Let us thank him because he did not despair of the republic. 7. The senate thanked me because I did not despair of the commonwealth. 8. He said that the senate would thank you because you did not despair of the commonwealth. 9. We ought to have thanked them because they surrounded our city with a wall. 10. We shall thank him because he has surrounded our city with a rampart and a ditch. 11. Let us go home and learn to speak Latin. 12. Who will teach us to speak

Latin? 13. Who is so stupid as not to wish to write Latin? 14. The Romans called Cicero the father of his country. 15. We shall elect this man consul. 16. If we elect him consul, he will be grateful to us. 17. Who of the Romans had the greatest influence? 18. Why did you stay so many years in that city? 19. Is this man very much to be feared? 20. No one of us has very great influence. 21. Did the night-guard of the Palatine move you in no respect? 22. This man is like me in countenance. 23. How old is this boy? 24. He is more than ten years old. 25. How deep is this river? 26. It is twenty-five feet deep.

XXXI.-XXXIV.

1. I shall not resign the praetorship. 2. No one can compel me to resign the praetorship. 3. Who would compel you to resign the praetorship? 4. If you should compel him to resign the praetorship, the senate would thank you. 5. We ought to free our city from the fear of slavery. 6. You could have released this city from blockade. 7. This wretch attempted to deprive us all of life. 8. Who has attempted to deprive you all of life? 9. We shall not be able to take possession of that city by a night-attack. 10. Our general will cross the river with all his troops. 11. We shall make use of both infantry and cavalry. 12. We employed his faithful service on that night. 13. I shall be glad to employ your service this day. 14. He says that a commander has been found worthy of the republic. 15. It happened that a commander was found worthy of the republic. 16. Can there be anything better than friendship? 17. Who is milder than I? 18. This man is much milder than you. 19. These

evils have spread more widely than we suppose. 20. We fear that this evil has spread more widely than we suppose. 21. You have lived in this city more than twenty years. 22. He has come with more than twenty thousand soldiers. 23. My country is much dearer to me than my life. 24. This man is of such a mind as to think that nothing is better than glory. 25. I can hire a house for one thousand sesterces. 26. He sold his house for twenty thousand sesterces. 27. This house will cost you twenty-five thousand sesterces. 28. Our fields excel yours in productiveness. 29. Since no one is hindering, we shall enter upon this war. 30. We entered upon that war without stirring up any public commotion. 31. We can make him resign his praetorship without stirring up any public commotion.

XXXV.-XXXVI.

1. You came to my house a little after midnight. 2. He came into the senate a little while ago. 3. We came to Marseilles day before yesterday. 4. A few days afterwards you set out from Rome. 5. This man came to Sicily ten days ago. 6. We think that Caius went six days before. 7. We shall stay at your house till late at night. 8. These men promised to kill me at my own house a little before daylight. 9. They came to my house on the following day a little before daylight. 10. We shall set out from Rome on the first of June. 11. You will set out on the fifteenth of March. 12. I think that he will come to the city on the thirteenth of September. 13. We shall stay in the vicinity of this city until you come. 14. There is no doubt that this general has performed great deeds both on land and sea. 15. They say that you

have performed great deeds both at home and in the field. 16. I have had a residence in Athens many years. 17. Since we have had a residence in America many years, the right of citizenship ought to be given us. 18. These wars were waged with much vicissitude on land and sea. 19. I fear that this war will be waged with much vicissitude both on land and sea. 20. This conspiracy can not be suppressed for all time. 21. Who can suppress this conspiracy for all time? 22. He asked the senate who could suppress that conspiracy for all time. 23. We hope to join that whole province to our government within twenty days. 24. The General annexed twenty cities to our government within one year.

XXXVII.-XL.

1. Shall we put up with this wretch who is longing to lay waste the earth? 2. Did you put up with him when he was making war upon his country? 3. Ought we to bear with him when he is desiring to set fire to our city? 4. Will you permit me to make use of an unusual style of speaking. 5. We permitted them to make use of an unusual style of speaking. 6. If you permit me to make use of an unusual style of speaking, I shall thank you. 7. These men staid at Rome for the purpose of killing the consuls. 8. Catiline staid at Rome for the purpose of killing the leading men of the state. 9. They will stay in the country for the purpose of killing me. 10. I fled from Athens for the purpose of saving myself. 11. Citizens fled from our city for the purpose of saving themselves. 12. We shall flee from home for the purpose of saving ourselves. 13. By reason of badly managing our business we have fallen into great debt. 14. We fear that

by reason of badly managing your business you will fall into great debt. 15. There is no doubt that he is likely to fall into great debt by reason of badly managing his business. 16. Let us not strengthen this conspiracy by not believing. 17. Do not strengthen this conspiracy by not believing. 18. You must not strengthen this conspiracy by keeping silent. 19. You could not have strengthened this conspiracy by keeping silent. 20. These men are preparing torches for firing the city. 21. Do not suffer them to prepare torches for firing our city. 22. You may prepare torches for firing this city. 23. You might have prepared torches for firing this city. 24. Are you intending to go home? 25. We were about to go into the country. 26. He is more likely to go to Athens than to Sicily. 27. You must decide to-day with respect to your own lives. 28. We had to decide on that day with respect to our lives. 29. He came to me to complain because the praetor was intending to send him into exile. 30. Many came to me on that day to pay their respects.

ENGLISH–LATIN VOCABULARY.

Numerals and Pronouns not given in this Vocabulary can be found in the Grammar. For Abbreviations see page xii. Words with definitions in SMALL CAPS are Synonymes.

A.

abandon, **relinquo, ĕre, līqui, lictum,** LEAVE BEHIND; **abjicio, jicĕre, jēci, jectum,** THROW FROM *or* AWAY.

able, am able, **possum, posse, potui.**

about, **circĭter,** *adv., used w. numerals;* **circum,** *prep. w. acc.*

absence, in one's absence, **absens,** *gen.* **absentis;** he was condemned in his absence, **absens damnātus est;** he came in your absence, **te absente venit.**

absent, **absens,** *gen.* **absentis.**

accept, **accipio, cipĕre, cēpi, ceptum.**

accordance, in accordance with, *see* L.N. XXXI., REF. 5–10.

account, on account of, **propter,** *prep. w. acc.*

accuse, **accūso, āre, āvi, ātum.**

accustomed, be accustomed, **soleo, ēre, solĭtus sum.**

acorn, **glans, glandis,** *f.*

acquainted, practically acquainted with, **perītus, a, um,** *w. gen.*

acquire, **compăro, āre, āvi, ātum,** BRING *or* PUT TOGETHER; **consĕquor, i, secūtus sum,** FOLLOW THOROUGHLY, FOLLOW CLOSE AFTER, REACH, OBTAIN.

across, **trans,** *prep. w. acc.*

act, **factum, i,** *n.*

address, **allŏquor, i, locūtus sum.**

adjust, **adjudĭco, āre, āvi, ātum.**

admonish, **admoneo, ēre, monui, monĭtum.**

adopt, **insisto, ĕre, stĭti,** *no sup.*

adorn, **orno, āre, āvi, ātum.**

advance, **progredior, grĕdi, gressus sum;** advance to the attack, **signa infĕro, inferre, intŭli, illātum.**

advice, ask advice of, *see under* ask.

advise, **moneo, ēre, ui, ĭtum.**

Aedui, **Aedui, ōrum,** *m. pl.*

affair, **res, rei,** *f.*

Africa, **Africa, ae,** *f.*
after, **postquam,** *conj.*
against, **in, contra,** *prep's w. acc.*
ago, a little while ago, **paulo ante;** ante *is an adverb; for* **paulo** *see* LN. XXXIII., REF. 7–9.
agree, **consentio, īre, sensi, sensum.**
agreeable, **gratus, a, um.**
aid, **auxilium, i,** *n.*
alarm, **commoveo, ēre, mōvi, mōtum.**
all, **omnis, e,** EVERY, THE WHOLE, ENTIRE, *pl.,* ALL (*persons*), ALL (*things*); **totus, a, um,** ALL THE, THE WHOLE, ENTIRE, TOTAL; **universus, a, um,** ALL *taken together,* WHOLE, ENTIRE, UNIVERSAL; **cuncti, ae, a,** ALL *united in a body,* ALL TOGETHER.
allay, **tolĕro, āre, āvi, ātum.**
Allobroges, **Allobrŏges, um,** *m. pl.*
ally, **socius, i,** *m.*
almost, **prope,** *adv.*
alone, **solus, a, um.**
Alps, **Alpes, ium,** *f. pl.*
already, **jam,** *adv.*
although, **quamquam, licet, cum (quum),** *conj's; see* LN. XIII.
always, **semper,** *adv.*
ambassador, **legātus, i,** *m.*
ambuscade, **insidiae, ārum,** *f. pl.*
America, **Amerĭca, ae,** *f.*
amid, **inter.** *prep. w. acc.*
among, **inter,** *prep. w. acc.;* **in,** *prep. w. abl. and acc.*
ancestors, **majōres, um,** *m. pl.*

and, **et, que, ac** *or* **atque,** *conj's.*
angry, be angry with, **irascor, i, irātus sum,** *w. dat.*
annex, **adjungo, ĕre, junxi, junctum.**
announce, **nuntio, āre, āvi, ātum.**
annoying, **molestus, a, um.**
another, **alius, a, ud.**
answer, **respondeo, ēre, spondi, sponsum.**
anxiety, **sollicitūdo (solicitūdo), ĭnis,** *f.*
anxious, **sollicĭtus (solicĭtus), a, um.**
any, anybody, anyone, anything, **alĭquis;** *in a negative sentence,* **ullus;** *after* **si, nisi, ne,** *and* **num, quis;** *for the declension see grammar under Indefinite Pron's; aft. prep.* **sine, ullus.**
Appian Way, **Appia Via, Appiae Viae,** *f.*
appoint, **indīco, ĕre, dixi, dictum,** DECLARE PUBLICLY, PROCLAIM; **constituo, ĕre, ui, ūtum,** PUT TOGETHER, ESTABLISH, ARRANGE.
approach, **appropinquo, āre, āvi, ātum,** COME NEAR TO, DRAW NIGH, *w. dat.;* **adeo, adīre, adīvi** *or* **adii, adĭtum,** GO TO, *w. acc.*
Aquitani, **Aquitāni, ōrum,** *m. pl.*
Aquitania, **Aquitania, ae,** *f.*
Ariovistus, **Ariovistus, i,** *m.*
arise, **coorior, īri, ortus sum.**
arms, **arma, ōrum,** *n. pl.*
army, **exercĭtus, us,** *m.*
arrival, **adventus, us,** *m.*

ARRIVE — BE AWAY.

arrive, **pervenio, īre, vēni, ventum.**
art, **ars, artis,** *f.*
as, **atque, ac,** *conj.;* as a deserter, **pro perfŭga, ae,** *m.*
as if, **velut, velut si, quam si,** *conj's; see* Ln. XII., Ref. 6.
as much ... as, **tantus ... quantus, a, um; tam ... quam.**
as soon as, **simul ac (atque); cum (quum) primum.**
as soon as possible, **quam primum,** *adv.*
ashamed, something causes one to be ashamed, **pudet, pudēre, puduit** *or* **pudĭtum est;** I am ashamed of the soldier, **me militis pudet.**
Asia, **Asia, ae,** *f.*
ask, **rogo, āre, āvi, ātum;** ask advice of, **consŭlo, ĕre, consului, consultum,** *w. acc.;* ask for, demand, **postŭlo, āre, āvi, ātum,** *w. acc.*
assassin, **sicarius, i,** *m.*
assault, make an assault, **signa inféro, inferre, intŭli, illātum;** to make an assault on the enemy, **in hostes signa inferre.**
assemble, **convenio, īre, vēni, ventum.**
assign, **attribuo, ĕre, tribui, tribūtum.**
at all, **omnīno,** *adv.*
at one and the same time, **simul,** *adv.;* at once, **statim,** *adv.*
at that time, **illo tempŏre,** *see* Ln. XXXV., Ref. 1–3; **id tempŏris,** *see* Ln. XXX., Ref. 1–6, *and* Ln. XXII., Ref. 6–8.

at the house of, **apud,** *prep. w. acc.*
Athenians, **Athenienses, ium,** *m. pl.*
Athens, **Athēnae, ārum,** *f. pl.*
attack, **impĕtus, us,** *m.;* to attack the enemy, **impĕtum in hostes facĕre.**
attack, **impetum facio, facĕre, feci, factum; ingredior, ingrĕdi, ingressus sum;** to attack the enemy, **in hostes impĕtum facĕre.**
attempt, **conor, āri, ātus sum.**
attend, give attention, **opĕram do, dăre, dĕdi, dătum.**
attentive, **attentus, a, um.**
auxiliaries, **auxilia, ōrum,** *n. pl.*
avert, **depello, ĕre, depŭli, depulsum.**
avoid, **vito, āre, āvi, ātum.**

B.

badly, **male,** *adv.*
baggage, **impedimenta, ōrum,** *n. pl.*
band, company, **manus, us,** *f.*
battle, **proelium, i,** *n.;* **pugna, ae,** *f.;* **pugna** *appears to be limited to a fight between individuals or armies.*
be able, can, **possum, posse, potui.**
be accustomed, be wont, **soleo, ēre, solĭtus sum.**
be angry with, **irascor, i, irātus sum,** *w. dat.*
be away, **absum, abesse, abfui.**

be born, descended, **nascor, i, natus sum.**
be in peril, **in pericŭlo versor, āri, ātus sum.**
be present, **adsum, adesse, adfui.**
be under obligation, **debeo, ēre, ui, ītum.**
be unoccupied, **vaco, āre, āvi, ātum.**
be unwilling, **nolo, nolle, nolui.**
be without, be deprived, **careo, ēre, ui, ītum.**
bear, **fero, ferre, tuli, latum;** bear with, **perfĕro, ferre, tŭli, lātum.**
because, **quod, quia,** *conj's.*
bed, **lectŭlus, i,** *m.*
before, **ante,** *prep. w. acc.;* **antĕquam, priusquam,** *conj's;* the night before, **superiōre nocte,** *see* Ln. XXXIV., Ref. 8-10.
beg, beg for, **oro, āre, āvi, ātum; peto, ĕre, īvi** *or* **ii, ītum.**
began, **coepi** *or* **coeptus sum, coepisse,** *defective verb;* **coeptus sum** *is only used with passive infinitives.*
begin, **incipio, cipĕre, cēpi, ceptum;** begin a battle, **proelium committo, ĕre, mīsi, missum.**
Belgians, **Belgae, ārum,** *m. pl.*
believe, **credo, ĕre, credĭdi, credĭtum.**
beseech, **quaeso, ĕre, īvi** *or* **ii,** *no sup.*
beset closely, **urgeo, urgueo, ēre, ursi,** *no. sup.*
besiege, **oppugno, āre, āvi, ātum.**

bestow, **impertio, īre, īvi** *or* **ii, ītum**
betake one's self, **se conferre; confĕro, conferre, contŭli, collātum.**
better, **melior, melius,** *gen.* **meliōris.**
beyond, across, **trans,** *prep. w. acc.;* beyond, more than, **praeter,** *prep. w. acc.*
blockade, **obsidio, ōnis,** *f.*
blood, **sanguis, sanguĭnis,** *m.*
boat, **linter, lintris,** *f.*
body, **corpus, corpŏris,** *n.*
boldness, **audacia, ae,** *f.*
born, be born, **nascor, i, natus sum.**
book, **liber, libri,** *m.*
both ... and, **et ... et.**
boy, **puer, i,** *m.*
brave, **fortis, e.**
bravely, **fortĭter,** *adv.*
break up camp, **castra moveo, ēre, movi, motum.**
briefly, a few things, **pauca, ōrum,** *n. pl.*
bridge, **pons, pontis,** *m.*
bring, bring to, **affĕro, afferre, attŭli, allātum.**
bring on, bring upon, **infĕro, inferre, intŭli, illātum;** to bring war upon the Gauls, **Gallis bellum inferre.**
bring to destruction, **ad exitium voco, āre, āvi, ātum.**
bring to pass, **efficio, ficĕre, fēci, fectum.**
Britons, **Britanni, ōrum,** *m. pl.*
brother, **frater, fratris,** *m.*
Brundisium, **Brundisium, i,** *n.*

business, **negotium, i,** *n.*
but, **sed, autem**; but if, **sin,** *conj's.*
butcher, **trucīdo, āre, āvi, ātum.**
by, **a, ab,** *prep. w. abl.*

C.

Caesar, **Caesar, ăris,** *m.*
call, **appello, āre, āvi, ātum,** ADDRESS, CALL *by name,* ENTITLE; **nomĭno, āre, āvi, ātum,** NAME, CALL *by name;* **voco, āre, āvi, ātum,** SUMMON, CALL *by name,* NAME.
camp, **castra, ōrum,** *n. pl.*
can, **possum, posse, potui**; cannot but, **facĕre non possum quin,** *w. subj.*
capability, **facultas, ātis,** *f.*
capital, **caput, ĭtis,** *n.*
capture, **capio, capĕre, cepi, captum.**
care, **cura, ae,** *f.*
care for, **provideo, ēre, vīdī, vīsum,** *w. dat.*
carefully, **diligenter,** *adv.*
carry on war, **bellum gero, ĕre, gessi, gestum.**
carry up, **subveho, ĕre, vexi, vectum.**
cart, **carrus, i,** *m.*
case, **causa, ae,** *f.;* **res, rei,** *f.*
Catiline, **Catilīna, ae,** *m.*
Catulus, **Catŭlus, i,** *m.*
cause, **causa, ae,** *f.;* cause, bring to pass, **efficio, ficĕre, fēci, fectum.**
cavalry, **equitātus, us,** *m.*
cease, **desĭno, ĕre, īvi** *or* **ii, ĭtum.**
censure, **accūso, āre, āvi, ātum.**
change, **commutatio, ōnis,** *f.*

check, **reprĭmo, ĕre, pressi, pressum.**
children, **libĕri, ōrum,** *m. pl.*
choose out, choose, **delĭgo, ĕre, lēgi, lectum.**
choose rather, **malo, malle, malui.**
Cicero, **Cicĕro, ōnis,** *m.*
Cilicia, **Cilicia, ae,** *f.*
citizen, **civis, is,** *m. and f.*
city, **urbs, urbis,** *f.*
class, **genus, ĕris,** *n.*
colony, **colonia, ae,** *f.*
come, **venio, īre, veni, ventum.**
comitium, **comitium, i,** *n.*
command, **impĕro, āre, āvi, ātum,** *w. dat.*
commander, **imperātor, ōris,** *m.*
commend, praise, **laudo, āre, āvi, ātum.**
common, **commūnis, e.**
commonwealth, **res publĭca, rei publĭcae,** *f.*
commotion, **tumultus, us,** *m.*
company, in company with, **cum,** *prep. w. abl.*
compassion, **misericordia, ae,** *f.*
compel, **cogo, ĕre, coēgi, coactum.**
complain, complain of, **queror, i, questus sum.**
condemn, **damno, āre, āvi, ātum.**
confer, talk with, **collŏquor, i, locūtus sum.**
conquer, **vinco, ĕre, vici, victum.**
consider, **habeo, ēre, ui, ĭtum.**
consign, intrust, **mando, āre, āvi, ātum.**
consists, **est** *w. pred. gen.* See LN. XXI., REF. 7-12.

conspiracy, **conjuratio, ōnis,** *f.*
conspirators, **conjurāti, ōrum,** *m. pl.*
consul, **consul, is,** *m.*; in the consulship of Metellus, **Metello consule;** see LN. XXXIV., REF. 11–16.
consular, **consulāris, e.**
consult, **consŭlo, ĕre, consului, consultum,** *w. acc.; w. dat.*, consult for, consult the interests of.
continually, **perpetuo,** *adv.*
contribute, **confĕro, conferre, contŭli, collātum.**
controversy, **controversia, ae,** *f.*
copiousness, **copia, ae,** *f.*
corn, **frumentum, i,** *n.*
cost, **sto, stare, steti, statum.**
council, **concilium, i,** *n.*
countenance, **os, oris,** *n.*
country, **terra, ae,** *f.*, LAND, EARTH, COUNTRY; **patria, ae,** *f.*, NATIVE COUNTRY, FATHERLAND; **rus, ruris,** *n.*, COUNTRY *as opposed to city;* into the country, **rus;** in the country, **ruri;** *see* LN. XXXVI.
courage, bravery, **virtus, ūtis,** *f.*
cowardly, **ignāvus, a, um.**
Crassus, **Crassus, i,** *m.*
crime, **scelus, ĕris,** *n.*
criminal, **facinorōsus, i,** *m.*
cross, **transeo, īre, īvi** *or* **ii, ītum.**
cruelty, **crudelĭtas, ātis,** *f.*
cultivate, **colo, ĕre, colui, cultum.**
custody, **custodia, ae,** *f.*
cut, cut down, **occīdo, ĕre, cīdi, cīsum,** STRIKE DOWN, CUT DOWN, KILL, SLAY; **interscindo, ĕre, scĭdi, scissum,** CUT ASUNDER, HEW TO PIECES, CUT DOWN.

D.

daily, **quotidiānus, a um.**
danger, **pericŭlum, i,** *n.*
dare, **audeo, ēre, ausus sum.**
darkness, **tenebrae, ārum,** *f. pl.*
day, **dies, ēi,** *m. and f.;* to-day, **hodie.**
daylight, a little before daylight, **paulo ante lucem.**
dear, **carus, a, um.**
death, **mors, mortis,** *f.*; put to death, **neco, āre, āvi, ātum.**
debt, **aes aliēnum, aeris aliēni,** *n.*
decide, **decerno, ĕre, crēvi, crētum,** *properly predicated of a public body or officer, as of a senate, or consul;* **dijudĭco, āre, āvi, ātum; judĭco, āre, āvi, ātum,** GIVE SENTENCE, DECIDE *as a judge;* be decided, **satis constat,** *w. dat. of person:* e. g. I am decided, **satis mihi constat.**
declare, **praedĭco, āre, āvi, ātum,** CRY IN PUBLIC, PROCLAIM; **indīco, ĕre, dixi, dictum,** DECLARE PUBLICLY, PUBLISH; to declare war against a city, **urbi bellum indicĕre.**
decree, **decerno, ĕre, crēvi, crētum;** decree of the senate, **senātus consultum, i,** *n.*
deed, **factum, i,** *n.*
deep, **altus, a, um.**

defend, **defendo, ĕre, fendi, fensum.**
defendant, **reus, i,** *m.*
delay, **moror, āri, ātus sum.**
demand, **postŭlo, āre, āvi, ātum;** I make this demand of him, **ab eo hoc postŭlo.**
denies, says not, **nego, āre, āvi, ātum.**
depart, **discēdo, ĕre, cessi, cessum; decēdo, ĕre, cessi, cessum.**
deprive, **privo, āre, āvi, ātum:** be deprived, **careo, ēre, ui, ĭtum.**
depth, **altitūdo, ĭnis,** *f.*
descended, be descended, **nascor, i, natus sum.**
deserter, as a deserter, **pro perfŭga.**
deserve, **mereor, ēri, merĭtus sum.**
deservedly, **merĭto,** *adv.*
design, **consilium, i,** *n.*
desire, **volo, velle, volui;** a desire, **voluntas, ātis,** *f.*
desolation, **vastĭtas, ātis,** *f.*
despair of, **despēro, āre, āvi, ātum;** *see* Ln. XXVIII., Ref. 4-8.
destroy, **deleo, ēre, ēvi, ētum.**
destruction, **exitium, i,** *n.*, A GOING OUT, GOING TO NOUGHT, RUIN; **interĭtus, us,** *m.*, A GOING AMONG *things so as to be no longer seen*, BECOMING LOST, GOING TO RUIN; **pernicies, ēi,** *f.*, KILLING UTTERLY, SLAUGHTER, OVERTHROW, DESTRUCTION.
determine, **statuo, ĕre, ui, ūtum.**

devastate, **vasto, āre, āvi, ātum.**
devote, **confĕro, conferre, contŭli, collātum.**
die, **morior, mori, mortuus sum.**
difficult, **difficĭlis, e.**
dignified, **gravis, e.**
direction, **pars, partis,** *f.*
disaster, **calamĭtas, ātis,** *f.*
disorder, throw into disorder, **perturbo, āre, āvi, ātum.**
disposition, **anĭmus, i,** *m.*
dispute, **controversia, ae,** *f.*
dissolve, **dimitto, ĕre, mīsi, missum.**
distant, be distant, **absum, abesse, abfui.**
distinguished, **egregius, a, um.**
district, **regio, ōnis,** *f.*
disturb, **perturbo, āre, āvi, ātum.**
disturbance, **tumultus, us,** *m.*
ditch, **fossa, ae,** *f.*
Divitiacus, **Divitiăcus, i,** *m.*
do, **facio, facĕre, feci, factum.**
do not, ETC., *see* Ln. V., Ref. 5-7.
doubt, **dubĭto, āre, āvi, ātum;** there is no doubt that, **non est dubium quin,** *w. subj.*
doubtful, **dubius, a, um.**
draw, delineate, **exprĭmo, ĕre, pressi, pressum;** draw up *troops,* **instruo, ĕre, struxi, structum.**
drive away, **depello, ĕre, depŭli, depulsum;** drive out, **expello, ĕre, expŭli, expulsum; ejicio, ejicĕre, ejēci, ejectum;** drive a ship, **navem defĕro, deferre, detŭli, delātum.**
due, be due, **debeor, ēri, debĭtus.**
Dumnorix, **Dumnŏrix, ĭgis,** *m.*

duty, **officium, i,** *n.*
dwell, dwell in, **incŏlo, ĕre, colui,** *no sup.*
dwelling, **domicilium, i,** *n.*

E.

eager, **appĕtens,** *gen.* **appetentis.**
earth, **orbis terrārum, orbis terrae; orbis, is,** *m.*
easily, **facĭle,** *adv.*
effective, be effective, **valeo, ēre, ui, ĭtum.**
effort, by his own effort, **per se.**
either . . . or, **aut . . . aut.**
elect, **creo, āre, āvi, ātum.**
employ, **utor, uti, usus sum; negotium, do, dare, dedi, datum;** I shall employ you to do this, **tibi negotium dabo ut hoc facias.**
encourage, **cohortor, āri, ātus sum,** EXHORT, ANIMATE, ADMONISH; **consōlor, āri, ātus sum,** COMFORT GREATLY, CHEER.
end, **finis, is,** *m.*
endeavor to bring about, **molior, īri, ītus sum.**
endure, **fero, ferre, tuli, latum; tolĕro, āre, āvi, ātum; subeo, īre, ii, ĭtum; perfĕro, ferre, tŭli, lātum.**
enemy, **hostis, is,** *m. and f.,* AN ENEMY *of one's country;* **inimīcus, i,** *m.,* A PERSONAL ENEMY.
English, **Angli, ōrum,** *m. pl.*
enjoyment, **fructus, us,** *m.*
enlist, **conscrībo, ĕre, scripsi, scriptum.**
enter upon, **ingrĕdior, ingrĕdi, ingressus sum;** I shall enter upon the war, **in bellum ingrediar.**
entire, **totus, a, um;** *see* all.
entreat, **oro, āre, āvi, ātum.**
envoy, **legātus, i,** *m.*
envy, **invideo, ēre, vīdi, vīsum.**
Ephesus, **Ephĕsus, i,** *f.*
especially, **praesertim,** *adv.*
establish, **constituo, ĕre, ui, ūtum.**
Etruria, **Etruria, ae,** *f.*
even if, **etiam si.**
evening, towards evening, **sub vespĕrum.**
ever, **semper,** ALWAYS; **umquam (unquam),** AT ANY TIME.
everlasting, **sempiternus, a, um.**
every one, **quisque, quaeque, quodque, quicque, quidque.**
evidence, **testimonium, i,** *n.*
evil, **malum, i,** *n.*
except, **praeter,** *prep. w. acc.*
excuse, **excūso, āre, āvi, ātum.**
exhort, **cohortor, āri, ātus sum.**
exile, **exsilium, i,** *n.*
exult, **exsulto (exulto), āre, āvi, ātum.**
eye, **ocŭlus, i,** *m.*

F.

face, **os, oris,** *n.*
face about, **signa converto, ĕre, verti, versum.**
fact, **res, rei,** *f.*
faithful, **fidēlis, e.**
fair, **pulcher, pulchra, pulchrum.**
fall into, **incĭdo, ĕre, cĭdi, cāsum.**
false, **falsus, a, um.**

fame, gloria, ae, *f.*
far, longe, *adv.*
farm revenues, vectigalia exerceo, ēre, ui, ĭtum.
father, pater, patris, *m.*
fault, culpa, ae, *f.*
fear, timor, ōris, *m.; ;* metus, us, *m.;* to fear, vereor, ēri, ĭtus sum; timeo, ēre, ui; metuo, ĕre, metui, metūtum.
fearless, fortis, e.
fearlessly, fortĭter, *adv.*
feel, have feeling, sentio, īre, sensi, sensum.
feel thankful, gratiam habeo, ēre, ui, ĭtum.
fellow-citizen, civis, is, *m.*
fertile, opīmus, a, um.
few, pauci, ae, a.
field, ager, agri, *m.;* in the field, militiae.
fifth, quintus, a, um.
fight, pugno, āre, āvi, ātum, used *impersonally in the passive:* e. g. pugnātur, it is fought, they fight.
find, invenio, īre, vēni, ventum, COME UPON, DISCOVER; reperio, ire, repĕri *and* reppĕri, repertum, MEET WITH, FIND OUT; cognosco, ĕre, cognōvi, cognĭtum, BECOME ACQUAINTED WITH, LEARN, KNOW.
finish, conficio, ficĕre, fēci, fectum.
fire, set on fire, inflammo, āre, āvi, ātum; with fire and sword, caede et incendiis.
firm, firmus, a, um.
firmly, firmĭter, *adv.*

first, primus, a, um; first to, first who, *see* LN. II., REF. 10–12.
fit, idoneus, a, um.
flee, fugio, fugĕre, fugi, fugĭtum; terga verto, ĕre, verti, versum.
fleet, classis, *f.*
flesh, caro, carnis, *f.*
flight, fuga, ae, *f.;* put to flight, in fugam do, dare, dedi, datum.
flow into, influo, ĕre, fluxi, fluxum.
follow, follow close after, subsĕquor, i, secūtus sum.
following, postĕrus, a, um.
fond, amans, *gen.* amantis.
foolish, stupid, amens, *gen.* amentis.
foot, pes, pedis, *m.*
footing, get a firm footing, *see* get.
for, pro, *prep. w. abl.;* nam, *conj.*
for a long time, now for a long time, jam diu, jam dudum, *adv's, see* LN. VI., REF. 3.
for the future, in relĭquum tempus.
for the most part, maxĭmam partem, *see* LN. XXX., REF. 1–6.
for the sake of, causa, *abl. and placed after its limiting gen.*
forbearance, venia, ae, *f.*
force, vis, vis, *f.;* by force, per vim; force, band, manus, us, *f.;* forces, troops, copiae, ārum, *f. pl.*
forest, silva, ae, *f.*
forget, obliviscor, i, oblītus sum.

forgetting, forgetfulness, oblivio, ōnis, *f.*
form, make, facio, facĕre, fēci, factum; form, draw up, instruo, ĕre, struxi, structum.
former, vetus, *gen.* vetĕris.
fort, castellum, i, *n.*
fortify, munio, īre, īvi, ītum.
found, build (*a city*), condo, ĕre, condĭdi, condĭtum.
four, quattuor.
France, Gallia, ae, *f.*
free, set free, libĕro, āre, āvi, ātum; free, liber, libĕra, libĕrum.
freely, libĕre, *adv.*
French, Galli, ōrum, *m. pl.*
frequent, frequens, *gen.* frequentis, REPEATED, OFTEN; creber, crebra, crebrum, THICK, CLOSE, NUMEROUS.
frequently, *often rendered by the adjective* frequens.
friend, amīcus, i, *m.*
friendship, amicitia, ae, *f.*
fright, terror, ōris, *m.*
from, out of, e, ex, *prep. w. abl.;* from, away from, from near, a, ab, abs, *prep. w. abl.*
fruit, fructus, us, *m.*
fruitful, fertĭlis, e.
full, plenus, a, um.
future, for the future, in relĭquum tempus.

G.

garrison, praesidium, i, *n.*
gate, porta, ae, *f.*
Gaul, Gallia, ae, *f.*
Gauls, Galli, ōrum, *m. pl.*

general, imperātor, ōris, *m.*
Geneva, Genāva, ae, *f.*
Germans, Germāni, ōrum, *m. pl.*
Germany, Germania, ae, *f.*
get a firm footing, firmĭter insisto, ĕre, instĭti, *no. sup.*
girl, puella, ae, *f.*
give, do, dare, dedi, datum; give back, reddo, ĕre, reddĭdi, reddĭtum; give up, abjicio, jicĕre, jēci, jectum.
glad, laetus, a, um.
glory, gloria, ae, *f.*
go, eo, īre, ivi, ĭtum; go back, redeo, redīre, redii, redĭtum; go to, adeo, adīre, adīvi *or* adii, adĭtum.
god, deus, dei, *m.*
good, bonus, a, um.
good-will, voluntas, ātis, *f.*
good health, be in good health, valeo, ēre, ui, ĭtum.
government, imperium, i, *n.*
governor, propraetor, ōris, *m.*; proconsul, is, *m.*
grant, do, dare, dedi, datum.
great, magnus, a, um; how great, quantus, a, um.
greatly, magnopĕre, *adv.*
greedy, avĭdus, a, um.
grieve for, doleo, ēre, ui, ĭtum, *see* LN. XXVIII., REF. 4-8.
guidance, under the guidance of the gods, diis ducĭbus, *see* LN. XXXIV., REF. 11-16.
guards, custodiae, ārum, *f. pl.*

H.

happens, it happens, comes to pass, the result is, accĭdit,

isse ; contingit, contigisse, contigit; fit, fieri, factum est; *these verbs are often used with a substantive clause as subject; see* LN. IX., REF. 4-8.

happy, beātus, a, um.

harbor, portus, us, *m.*

hasten, make haste, matūro, āre, āvi, ātum; contendo, ĕre, tendi, tentum.

hated, to be hated, in odio esse, *w. dat. of person by whom hated.*

have, habeo, ēre, ui, ĭtum.

have power, influence, valeo, ēre, ui, ĭtum ; to have very great influence, plurĭmum valēre.

he, she, it, is, ea, id.

health, be in good health, valeo, ēre, ui, ĭtum.

hear, audio, īre, īvi, ĭtum.

heart, cor, cordis, *n., the physical organ; also* THE HEART *as the seat of feeling;* anĭmus, THE SOUL *considered as the seat of feeling,* FEELING, HEART.

help, succurro, ĕre, succurri, succursum.

Helvetia, Helvetia, ae, *f.*

hesitate, dubĭto, āre, āvi, ātum.

hide, obscūro, āre, āvi, ātum.

high-born, nobĭlis, e.

highest, summus, a, um.

hill, collis, is, *m.*

hinder, impedio, īre, īvi *or* ii, ītum, ENTANGLE, EMBARRASS, HINDER ; reprĭmo, ĕre, pressi, pressum, PRESS BACK, KEEP BACK, RESTRAIN, HINDER.

hire, condūco, ĕre, duxi, ductum.

his, her, its, suus, a, um, *when referring to the same person or thing as the subject of its sentence, otherwise* ejus ; *see* LN. III.

historian, rerum auctor, *or* rerum scriptor.

hither, on this side, near, citerior, citerius, *gen.* citeriōris.

hitherto, adhuc, *adv.*

hold, teneo, ēre, ui, tentum.

home, homeward, domum; at home, domi ; *see* LN. XXXVI.

honor, honor, ōris, *m.*

hope, spes, spei, *f.;* to hope, spero, āre, āvi, ātum.

horse, equus, i, *m.*

hostage, obses, obsĭdis, *m. and f.*

hostile, infestus, a, um.

hot, fervĭdus, a, um.

house, domus, us, *f., the generic word;* tectum, i, *n., that which covers,* THE ROOF, *by metonymy* HOUSE ; at the house of, apud, *prep. w. acc.*

hover, versor, āri, ātus sum.

how great, quantus, a, um.

how many, quot, *indecl. adj.;* quam multi, ae, a.

however, however much, quamvis, *conj.*

hunger, fames, is, *f.*

hurl, conjicio, jicĕre, jēci, jectum.

I.

I, ego, mei.

if, si, *conj.;* if only, modo, dum, dum modo, *conj's.*

ignorant, ignārus, a, um.

illustrious, **clarus, a, um.**
imitate, **imĭtor, āri, ātus sum.**
immortal, **immortālis, e.**
impious, **nefarius, a, um.**
in, **in,** *prep. w. abl.*
in behalf of, **pro,** *prep. w. abl.*
in no ordinary manner, **non mediocrĭter,** *adv.*
in no respect, **nihil,** *see* LN. XXX., REF. 1-6.
in order to, *see* LN. VII., NOTE 1.
in person, **coram,** *adv.*
in the meantime, **intĕrim,** *adv.*
in the vicinity of, **ad,** *prep. w. acc.*
in what manner, **quemadmŏdum,** *adv.*
inactivity, **inertia, ae,** *f.*
incite, **inflammo, āre, āvi, ātum.**
increase, **augeo, ēre, auxi, auctum,** *transitive;* **cresco, ĕre, crevi, cretum,** *intransitive.*
indeed, at least, **quidem,** *adv., placed immediately after the emphatic word.*
induce, **addūco, ĕre, duxi, ductum.**
industrious, **studiōsus, a, um.**
inevitable, **inevitabĭlis, e.**
infantry, **pedĭtes, um,** *m. pl.*
inflict punishment, **supplicium sumo, ĕre, sumpsi, sumptum;** to inflict punishment on a soldier, **de milĭte supplicium sumĕre.**
influence, **auctorītas, ātis,** *f.;* have influence, exert influence, **valeo, ēre, ui, ĭtum.**
inform anyone, **alĭquem certiōrem facio, facere, feci, factum;** be informed, **certior fio, fiĕri, factus sum.**
inquire, **quaero, ĕre. quaesīvi** *or* **quaesii, quaesītum.**
intrust, **commendo, āre, āvi, ātum.**
into, **in,** *prep. w. acc.*
invested, **occupātus, a, um.**
invite, send for, **arcesso, ĕre, arcessīvi, arcessītum; invīto, āre, āvi, ātum.**
island, **insŭla, ae,** *f.*
it, **is, ea, id.**
it is allowed, it is permitted, one may, **licet, licēre, licuit** *or* **licĭtum est,** *see* LN. XVII., Ex's 14, 15.
it is of importance, it matters, it concerns, **interest, esse, fuit,** *see* LN. XXIV., REF. 12-14.
it is proper, it behooves, one ought, **oportet, oportēre, oportuit,** *see* LN. XVII., Ex's 16, 17.
it is the duty of, part of, **est** *w. pred. gen., see* LN. XXI., REF. 7-12.
it is unavoidable, it is necessary, one must, **necesse est,** *see* LN. XVII., Ex. 18; **necesse** *is an indecl. adj.*
Italy, **Italia, ae,** *f.*

J.

join to, annex, **adjungo, ĕre, junxi, junctum.**
join together, unite, **conjungo, ĕre, junxi, junctum.**
journey, **iter, itinĕris,** *n.;* to journey, **iter facio, facĕre, feci, factum.**

judge, **judex, judĭcis,** *m.*
July, of July, **Quintīlis, e,** *adj.*
Jupiter Stator, **Juppĭter Stator, Jovis Statōris,** *m.*
just, **aequus, a, um.**
justice, **aequĭtas, ātis,** *f.*
justly, **jure,** *abl. of manner.*

K.

keep, preserve, **asservo, āre, āvi, ātum** ; keep, hold, **habeo, ēre. ui, ītum** ; keep, restrain, **contineo, ēre, ui, tentum** ; keep in line, **ordĭnes servo, āre, āvi, ātum.**
keeper, **custos, ōdis,** *m.*
kill, **interficio, ficĕre, fēci, fectum.**
kindness, **beneficium, i,** *n.*, FAVOR, SERVICE, *something done for another;* **humanĭtas, ātis,** *f.*, PHILANTHROPIC BEHAVIOR, PHILANTHROPY, HUMANITY : **humanĭtas** *describes a person's character;* **beneficium,** *his act.*
king, **rex, regis,** *m.*
know, know how, **scio, scire, scivi** *or* **scii, scitum** ; not know, **nescio, īre, īvi** *or* **ii, ītum.**

L.

land, **terra, ae,** *f.*
large, **magnus, a, um.**
last, last part of, **extrēmus, a, um** ; last year, **proxĭmus annus.**
late, till late at night, **ad multam noctem.**

lately, **nuper.** *adv.*
Latin, speak Latin, **Latīne loquor, i, locūtus sum.**
Lavinium, **i,** *n.*
law, **lex, legis,** *f.*, BILL, ENACTMENT, STATUTE ; **jus, juris,** *n.*, RIGHT, LAW, *whether natural, human, or divine; written or unwritten; also* STATUTE LAW, CONSTITUTIONAL LAW, *considered as a whole;* **lex** *refers to a particular enactment.*
lay violent hands on, **vim et manus infĕro, inferre, intŭli, illātum,** *see* LN. XXVI., NOTE 3.
lay waste, **vasto, āre, āvi, ātum.**
lead, **duco, ĕre, duxi, ductum** ; lead across, **tradūco, ĕre, duxi, ductum** ; lead down, **dedūco, ĕre, duxi, ductum** ; lead out, **edūco, ĕre, duxi, ductum** ; lead to, **addūco, ĕre, duxi, ductum.**
leader, **dux, ducis,** *m. and f.*
leading men, **princĭpes, um,** *m. pl.*
learn, **cognosco, ĕre, cognōvi, cognĭtum.**
leave behind, leave, **relinquo, ĕre, līqui, lictum.**
leave off, cease, **desĭno, ĕre, desīvi** *or* **desii, desĭtum.**
left, **sinister, sinistra, sinistrum.**
legate, **legātus, i,** *m.*
legion, **legio, ōnis,** *f.*
leisure, **otium, i,** *n.*
less, **minor, minus** ; *gen.* **minōris.**
lessen, **levo, āre, āvi, ātum.**

let us, him, ETC., *see* LN. V., REF. 3, 4.
letter, **littĕrae, ārum,** *f. pl.*
lie in wait, **insidior, āri, ātus sum.**
lieutenant, **legātus, i,** *m.*
life, **vita, ae,** *f.*
light, daylight, **lux, lucis,** *f.;* a little before daylight, **paulo ante lucem.**
like, **simĭlis,** e.
likewise, **idem;** *see* LN. IV., REF. 1-8, Ex. 5.
line, line of battle, **acies, ēi,** *f.*
little, **parvus, a, um.**
live, **vivo, ĕre, vixi, victum; vitam dego, ĕre, degi,** *no. sup.*
long, long for, desire eagerly, **cupio, cupĕre, cupīvi** *or* **cupii, cupītum.**
long, a long time, longer, longest, **diu, diutius, diutissĭme,** *adv.*
long, **longus, a, um.**
long since, **jam pridem,** *adv.*
look at, **intueor, ēri, intuītus sum.**
love, **amor, ōris,** *m.;* to love, **amo, āre, āvi, ātum.**
Lucullus, **Lucullus, i,** *m.*

M.

madness, **furor, ōris,** *m.*
magistrate, **magistrātus, us,** *m.*
maintain, **retineo, ēre, tinui, tentum.**
make, **facio, facĕre, feci, factum;** make an assault, *see* assault; make requital, **gratiam**
refĕro, referre, retŭli, relātum. — I shall requite you, **tibi gratiam refĕram;** make upon, **infĕro, inferre, intŭli, illātum.** — to make war upon the Gauls, **Gallis bellum inferre;** make use of, **utor, uti, usus sum,** *w. abl.*
man, **vir, viri,** *m.,* A MAN *as distinguished from a woman;* **homo, ĭnis,** *m. and f.,* MAN, A HUMAN BEING.
manage, **gero, gerĕre, gessi, gestum.**
many, **multi, ae, a;** many times, **saepe.**
Marcellus, **Marcellus, i,** *m.*
march, **iter, itinĕris,** *n.;* to march, **iter facio, facĕre, feci, factum;** on the march, *see under* on the march.
Marcus, **Marcus, i,** *m.*
Marius, **Marius, i,** *m.*
Marseilles, **Massilia, ae,** *f.*
massacre, **internecio, ōnis,** *f.*
may, *see* LN, XVII., Ex. 14.
meantime, in the meantime, **intĕrim,** *adv.*
meet, to meet, **se obvium ferre;** you met me, **mihi te obvium tulisti;** go to meet, **obviam** (*or* **obvius, a. um**) **eo, ire, ivi, itum;** I shall go to meet you, **tibi obvius ibo;** meet with, **invenio, īre, vēni, ventum,** *w. acc.*
memory, within the memory of man, **post homĭnum memoriam.**
mercy, **misericordia, ae,** *f.*

messenger, **nuntius, i,** *m.*
Metellus, **Metellus, i,** *n.*
middle, middle of, **medius, a, um.**
midnight, a little after midnight, **paulo post mediam noctem.**
midst of, **medius, a, um.**
mild, **mitis, e.**
mile, **mille passuum.**
military affairs, **res militāris, rei militāris.**
milk, **lac, lactis,** *n.*
mind, **mens, mentis,** *f.*, UNDERSTANDING, INTELLECT, REASON; **anĭmus, i,** *m.*, WILL, DESIRE, PURPOSE; FEELING, AFFECTION, SENTIMENT.
misfortune, **calamĭtas, ātis,** *f.*
moment, **punctum, i,** *n.*
money, **pecunia, ae,** *f.*
more, **plus, pluris,** *n.;* **amplius, magis,** *adv's.*
Moselle, **Mosella, ae,** *m. and f.*
mother, **mater, matris,** *f.*
mountain, **mons, montis,** *m.*
move, **moveo, movēre, movi, motum.**
much, **multus, a, um.**
multitude, **multitūdo, ĭnis,** *f.*
murder, *see* kill.
murderer, **sicarius, i,** *m.*
my, **meus, a, um.**

N.

name, **nomen, nomĭnis,** *n.;* to name, *see* call.
Naples, **Neapŏlis, is,** *f.*
narrow, contracted, small, **parvus, a, um;** narrow limits, **angustiae, ārum,** *f. pl.*

nation, **natio, ōnis,** *f.;* **gens, gentis,** *f.*
nature, **natūra, ae,** *f.*
near, **prope,** *adv.*
nearest, **proxĭmus, a, um.**
nearly, **paene,** *adv.*
need, **indigeo, ēre, ui,** *no sup.*
negligence, **nequitia, ae,** *f.*
neighborhood, in the neighborhood of, **ad,** *prep. w. acc.*
neighbors, **finitĭmi, ōrum,** *m. pl.*
neither ... nor, **neque ... neque, nec ... nec.**
never, **numquam (nunquam),** *adv.*
nevertheless, yet, still, **tamen,** *adv.*
new, **novus, a, um.**
night, **nox, noctis,** *f.;* night before, **nox superior;** till late at night, **ad multam noctem.**
night-attack, **nocturnus impĕtus; nocturnus, a, um; impĕtus, us,** *m.*
night-guard, **nocturnum praesidium; nocturnus, a, um; praesidium, i,** *n.*
no, **nullus, a, um.**
nobody, no one, **nemo,** *gen. and dat. supplied from* **nullus.**
not, **non, ne,** *adv.;* not even, **ne ... quidem,** *w. the emphatic word between* **ne** *and* **quidem;** not one slave, **nemo servus;** nor, **neque, neve,** *conj's.*
not only ... but also, **non solum ... sed etiam.**
not yet, **nondum,** *adv.*
nothing, **nihil.**
now, **nunc, jam,** *adv's.*

number, **numĕrus, i,** *m.;* in great numbers, **frequentes,** *see* Ln. II., Ref. 10–12.

numerous, **creber, crebra, crebrum.**

O.

obey, **pareo, ēre, ui, ĭtum.**
observe, **cognosco, ĕre, cognōvi, cognĭtum.**
occupy, **occŭpo, āre, āvi, ātum.**
of such a kind, of such a character, **ejus modi.**
offend, **offendo, ĕre, fendi, fensum.**
offer, **offĕro, offerre, obtŭli, oblātum.**
office, **munus, munĕris,** *n.*
often, **saepe,** *adv.*
old, **senex,** *gen.* **senis**; old, *having been born*, **natus, a, um**; he is twenty years old, **vigĭnti annos natus est.**
on, **in,** *prep. w. acc. aft. verbs of motion, w. abl. aft. verbs of rest.*
on account of, **propter,** *prep. w. acc.*
on the march, **ex itinĕre, in itinĕre**; to storm a town on the march, **oppĭdum ex itinĕre expugnāre**; to be on the march, **in itinĕre esse.**
on this side of, **cis,** *prep. w. acc.*
once, at once, **statim,** *adv.*
one, **unus, a, um.**
only person who, *see* Ln. X., Ref. 1–9 *and* Ex. 7.
opinion, **sententia, ae,** *f.,* OPINION, DECISION, SENTENCE, JUDGMENT; **opinio, ōnis,** *f.,* OPINION, SUPPOSITION, CONJECTURE, BELIEF.
opportunity, **occasio, ōnis,** *f.*
or, **aut**; *in double questions,* **an.**
or not, *in direct double questions,* **an non**; *in indirect double questions,* **necne.**
orator, **orātor, ōris,** *m.*
order, in order that, **ut,** *conj.; see* Ln. VII., Note 1.
order, by order, **jussu,** *abl. sing. m.*
order, command, **jubeo, ēre, jussi, jussum.**
ordinary, in no ordinary manner, **non mediocrĭter,** *adv.*
ought, **debeo, ēre, ui, ĭtum**; debeo *denotes a moral obligation; see also* Ln. XVII., Ex's 16 *and* 17.
our, **noster, nostra, nostrum.**
out of, **e, ex,** *prep. w. abl.*
overcome, **supĕro, āre, āvi, ātum.**
own, *see* Ln. III., Ref. 3–7.

P.

pace, **passus, us,** *m.;* a thousand paces, a mile, **mille passuum.**
pain, **dolor, ōris,** *m.*
Palatine, **Palatium, i,** *n.*
pardon, **ignosco, ĕre, ignōvi, ignōtum.**
part, **pars, partis,** *f.;* for the most part, **maxĭmam partem,** *see* Ln. XXX., Ref. 1–6.
participant, **particeps,** *gen.* **particĭpis,** *adj.*
pass the winter, **hiĕmo, āre, āvi, ātum.**

patriotic, **bonus, a, um.**
pay, **pendo, ĕre, pependi, pensum**; pay one's respects, **salūto, āre, āvi, ātum.**
peace, **pax, pacis,** *f.*
perform, **fungor, fungi, functus sum,** EXECUTE, DISCHARGE, OBSERVE; **gero, ĕre, gessi, gestum,** MANAGE, WAGE, TRANSACT, ACCOMPLISH.
perhaps, **fortasse,** *adv.*
peril, **pericŭlum, i,** *n.;* be in peril, **in pericŭlo versor, āri, ātus sum.**
perilous, **periculōsus, a, um.**
perish, **pereo, īre, ii, ĭtum.**
permission, *see* LN. XVII., EX. 5.
permit, allow, suffer, **patior, pati, passus sum.**
persuade, **persuadeo, suadēre, suāsi, suāsum.**
pirate, **praedo, ōnis,** *m.*
pitch a camp, **castra pono, ĕre, posui, posĭtum.**
pity, **misereor, ēre, miserĭtus sum; misĕret, miserēre, miseruit,** *see* LN. XXIV., REF. 4–8.
place, **locus, i,** *m.; pl.* **loci** *and* **loca, locōrum,** *m. and n.;* take place, **geror, i, gestus sum.**
plan, **consilium, i,** *n.,* DETERMINATION, RESOLUTION, PURPOSE; **ratio, ōnis,** *f.,* COURSE, MANNER, METHOD, FASHION.
please, **delecto, āre, āvi, ātum,** *w. acc.;* **placeo, ēre, ui, ĭtum,** *w. dat.*
pleasing, **gratus, a, um.**
plot, **cogĭto, āre, āvi, ātum.**

Pompey, **Pompēius, i,** *m.*
poor, **pauper,** *gen.* **paupĕris.**
portray, **exprĭmo, ĕre, pressi, pressum.**
portraiture, **imāgo, ĭnis,** *f.*
possession, **possessio, ōnis,** *f. ; often omitted after possessive pronouns:* e. g. he surrenders himself and *his possessions,* **se suaque dat;** take possession of, **occŭpo, āre, āvi, ātum,** *w. acc.*
powerful, **potens,** *gen.* **potentis.**
practically acquainted with, **perītus, a, um,** *w. gen.*
practice, **exercitatio, ōnis,** *f.*
praetor, **praetor, ōris** *m.*
praetorship, **praetūra, ae,** *f.*
praise, **laus, laudis,** *f.;* to praise, **laudo, āre, āvi, ātum.**
pray, **quaeso, ĕre, īvi** *or* **ii, ĭtum**; pray, who? pray, what? **quis tandem? quid tandem?**
prefer, **malo, malle, malui; antepōno, ĕre, posui, posĭtum**: I prefer my country to your city, **tuae urbi patriam meam antepōno;** I prefer going to staying, **ire malo quam remanēre.**
preparation, **comparatio, ōnis,** *f.*
prepare, **paro, āre, āvi, ātum.**
prepared, **parātus, a, um.**
present, **dono, āre, āvi, ātum.**
present, be present, **adsum, adesse, adfui.**
prevent, **deterreo, ēre, ui, ĭtum.**
private property, **res familiāris, rei familiāris,** *f.*
privilege, power, **potestas, ātis,** *f.*

productiveness, **ubertas, ātis,** *f.*
promise, **polliceor, ēri, pollicĭtus sum.**
proper, **idoneus, a, um.**
property, **res, rerum,** *f. pl.;* **bona, ōrum,** *n. pl.; often omitted after possessive pronouns;* private property, **res familiāris, rei familiāris,** *f.*
prosperous, **florens,** *gen.* **florentis.**
prosperity, *see* welfare.
protection, **praesidium, i,** *n.;* to protect any one, **alicui praesidio esse,** *see* L_N. XXVII., R_EF. 1-3; to protect *with fortifications, guards, etc.,* **munio, ire, ivi, itum.**
provide for, **provideo, ēre, vīdi, vīsum.**
provided that, **modo, dum, dum modo,** *conj's.* See L_N. XII., R_EF. 8.
province, **provincia, ae,** *f.*
provision, make provision, **provideo, ēre, vīdi, vīsum.**
provoke, exasperate, enrage, **lacesso, ĕre, īvi** *or* **ii, ītum.**
publicly, **publĭce,** *adv.*
punish, **punio, īre, ivi** *or* **ii, ītum.**
punishment, **supplicium, i,** *n.;* to inflict punishment upon any one, **de aliquo supplicium sumo, ĕre, sumpsi. sumptum;** to suffer punishment, **poenas persolvo, ĕre, solvi, solūtum.**
purpose, for the purpose of, **causa,** *abl. of cause and stands after its limiting genitive.*
put around, **circumdo, dăre,** **dĕdi, dătum,** *see* L_N. XXV., R_EF. 4-5.
put to death, **neco, āre, āvi, ātum.**
put to flight, in fugam do, dare, dedi, datum; **fugo, āre, āvi, ātum.**
put up with, bear with, endure, **perfĕro, perferre, pertŭli, perlātum.**

Q.

quarrel, **dissentio, ōnis,** *f.*
question, **quaestio, ōnis,** *f.*
Quintus, **Quintus, i,** *m.*

R.

raft, **ratis, is,** *f.*
rage, **furor, ōris,** *m.*
rampart, **vallum, i,** *n.*
ravage, **popŭlor, āri, ātus sum.**
reach, **capio, capĕre, cepi, captum.**
read, **lego, ĕre, legi, lectum.**
receive, **accipio, cipĕre, cēpi, ceptum.**
recover, **recupĕro, āre, āvi, ātum; recipio, cipĕre, cēpi, ceptum,** *w. reflexive pronoun.*
refuse, **recūso, āre, āvi, ātum.**
regard as an enemy, **pro hoste habeo, ēre, ui, ītum.**
reign, **regno, āre, āvi, ātum.**
rejoice, **exsulto, (exulto), āre āvi, ātum,** REJOICE EXCEEDINGLY, RUN RIOT, REVEL, EXULT; **laetor, āri, ātus sum,** FEEL JOY, BE VERY GLAD, BE JOYFUL.

release, **libĕro, āre, āvi, ātum**.
relieve, **libĕro, āre, āvi, ātum**.
remaining, **relĭquus, a, um**.
remains, it remains, **restat**; **relĭquum est**.
remember, **memĭni, meminisse**.
remind, **admoneo, ēre, ui, ĭtum**.
renew, **redintegro, āre, āvi, ātum**.
renown, **gloria, ae,** *f.*
repeat, **repĕto, ĕre, īvi** *or* **ii, ĭtum**.
repent, **paenĭtet, ēre, paenituit**, *see* L<small>N</small>. XXIV., R<small>EF</small>. 4–8.
reply, **respondeo, ēre, spondi, sponsum**.
report, **rumor, ōris,** *m.*; to report, **nuntio, āre, āvi, ātum**, <small>ANNOUNCE, DECLARE, MAKE KNOWN</small>; **refĕro, referre, retŭli, relātum**, <small>BRING BACK, RELATE, RECITE, REPEAT</small>.
reprimand, **accūso, āre, āvi, ātum**.
request, **postulatio, ōnis,** *f.*
requite, make requital, *see under* make.
rescue, **eripio, eripĕre, eripui, ereptum**.
residence, **domicilium, i,** *n.*
resign, **abdĭco, āre, āvi, ātum**; he has resigned the praetorship, **se praetūrā abdicāvit**.
respect, in no respect, **nihil**; *see* L<small>N</small>. XXX., R<small>EF</small>. 1–6.
rest of, **relĭquus, a um**; the rest, **cetĕri, a, um**.
restrain, **reprĭmo, ĕre, pressi, pressum**; **retineo, ēre, tinui, tentum**.

result, the result is, **accĭdit**; **fit**; *see* L<small>N</small>. IX., R<small>EF</small>. 4–8.
retain, hold, **teneo, ēre, ui, tentum**.
return, **revertor, i, versus sum**; **reverto, ĕre, reverti**; *the present, imperfect, and future tenses have the passive form; the perfect, pluperfect, and future perfect the active form;* **redeo, ĭre, ii, ĭtum**.
revenue, **vectīgal, ālis,** *n.*
reward, **remunĕror, āri, ātus sum**.
Rhine, **Rhenus, i,** *m.*
right, **jus, juris,** *n.*; **dexter, dextra, dextrum,** *adj.*
river, **flumen, flumĭnis,** *n.*
road, **via, ae,** *f.*
rob, **spolio, are, āvi, ātum**.
rock, **saxum, i,** *n.*
Roman, **Romānus, a, um**.
Rome, **Roma, ae,** *f.*
rouse, **inflammo, āre, āvi, ātum**.
rout, **fugo, āre, āvi, ātum**.
rudiments, **elementa, ōrum,** *n. pl.*
rule over, **impĕro, āre, āvi, ātum,** *w. dat.*
run, **curro, ĕre, cucurri, cursum**, run riot, **exsulto, āre, āvi, ātum**.

S.

safe, **tutus, a, um,** <small>WELL GUARDED, SECURE, OUT OF DANGER</small>; **salvus, a, um,** <small>UNHARMED, UNINJURED, WELL, SOUND</small>.
safely, **tuto**.

safety, **salus, ūtis,** *f.*
sail, **navĭgo, āre, āvi, ātum.**
sake, for the sake of, **causā.**
sally, **excursio, ōnis,** *f.*
same, the same, **idem.**
satisfied, **contentus, a, um.**
satisfy, **satisfacio, facĕre, fēci, factum.**
savageness, **atrocĭtas, ātis,** *f.*
save, **servo, āre, āvi, ātum;** con**servo, āre, āvi, ātum;** con**servo** *is* **servo** *intensified by the prefix* **con** *and properly signifies* KEEP THOROUGHLY, SAVE COMPLETELY.
say, **dico, dicĕre, dixi, dictum;** say not, **nego, āre, āvi, ātum.**
scatter, rout, **fugo, āre, āvi, ātum.**
scout, **explorātor, ōris,** *m.*
sea, **mare, maris,** *n.*
seize, **occŭpo, āre, āvi, ātum.**
see, **video, ēre, vidi, visum.**
seem, **videor, ēri, visus sum.**
self, **ipse, a, um.**
sell, **vendo, ĕre, vendĭdi, vendĭtum.**
senate, **senātus, us,** *m.*
senator, **senātor, ōris,** *m.*
send, **mitto, ĕre, misi, missum.**
send for, cause to come, **arcesso, ĕre, arcessīvi, arcessītum.**
send forward, **praemitto, ĕre, mīsi, missum.**
separate, **sejungo, ĕre, junxi, junctum.**
Sequani, **Sequăni, ōrum,** *m. pl.*
serve, **servio, īre, īvi, ītum.**
service, aid, **opĕra, ae,** *f.*
set fire to, **incendo, ĕre, cendi, censum.**

sesterce, **sestertius, i,** *m.; a small silver coin worth nearly four cents.*
set forth, **propōno, ĕre, posui, posĭtum.**
set out, march, depart, **proficiscor, i, profectus sum.**
settle, **consīdo, ĕre, sēdi, sessum.**
seventh, **septĭmus, a, um.**
severe, **gravis, e.**
severely, **gravĭter,** *adv*
ship, **navis, is,** *f.*
short, **brevis, e.**
shout, **clamor, ōris,** *m.*
show, **doceo, ēre, ui, doctum.**
shudder at, **horreo, ēre,** *no perf. nor sup., governs acc.;* shudder greatly at, **perhorresco, ĕre, horrui,** *no sup., governs acc.*
Sicily, **Sicilia, ae,** *f.*
sick, **aeger, aegra, aegrum.**
side, on this side of, **cis,** *prep. w. acc.*
siege, **oppugnatio, ōnis,** *f.*
sight, **conspectus, us,** *m.*
signal, **signum, i,** *n.*
Silanus, **Silānus, i,** *m.*
silent, keep silent, **taceo, ēre, ui, ĭtum.**
since, **cum (quum), quoniam,** *conj's.; see* LN. XIV., REF. 1-5.
singularly, **egregie,** *adv.*
sixty, **sexaginta.**
size, **magnitūdo, ĭnis,** *f.*
skilful, practically acquainted with, **perītus, a, um,** *see* LN. XXIII., REF. 6-12.
slaughter, **occīdo, ĕre, cīdi, cīsum.**

slave, **servus, i,** *m.*
slavery, **servītus, ūtis,** *f.*
small, **parvus, a, um.**
so, **tam, ita, sic,** *adv's;* so great, **tantus, a, um;** so very much, **tam vehementer.**
so as to, *see* L<small>N</small>. IX., N<small>OTE</small> 1.
soldier, **miles, milĭtis,** *m.*
some one, something, some, **alĭquis, quidam, nescio quis;** *see* L<small>N</small>. IV., R<small>EF</small>. 9–13.
some . . . others, **alii . . . alii.**
son, **filius, i,** *m.*
son-in-law, **gener, genĕri,** *m.*
soon, as soon as possible, **quam primum.**
sorrow, **dolor, ōris,** *m.*
sound, healthy, well, **sanus, a, um.**
speak, **loquor, i, locūtus sum; dico, ĕre, dixi, dictum.**
spirit, **anĭmus, i,** *m.*
spiritedly, **acrĭter,** *adv.;* to make a spirited assault, **acrĭter signa inferre.**
spoils, **spolia, ōrum,** *n. pl.*
spread, **dissemĭno, āre, āvi, ātum.**
spread abroad, **perfĕro, perferre, pertŭli, perlātum.**
stand, **sto, stare, steti, statum.**
stand about, stand around, **circumsto, stāre, stĕti, stătum.**
standard, **signum, i,** *n.*
stake, (something) is at stake, **agĭtur.**
state, **res publĭca, rei publĭcae,** *f.*
stay, **remaneo, ēre, mansi,** *no sup.*
still, **etiam nunc, tamen,** *adv's.*

stir up, **concĭto, āre, āvi, ātum.**
storm, **expugno, āre, āvi, ātum;** a storm, tempest, **tempestas, ātis,** *f.*
story, **fabŭla, ae,** *f.*
stranger, **aliēnus, i,** *m.*
straw, not to care a straw for any one, **alĭquem flocci non facĕre.**
strengthen, **corrobŏro, āre, āvi, ātum.**
strong, **firmus, a, um.**
stupid, **stultus, a, um; amens,** *gen.* **amentis.**
style, **genus, genĕris,** *n.*
submit to, **subeo, īre, ii, ĭtum,** *w. acc.*
such, so great, **tantus, a, um;** such, of such a kind, **talis, e;** such . . . as, **tantus . . . quantus,** *when referring to size;* **talis . . . qualis** *when referring to kind, nature, quality.*
suddenly, **subĭto,** *adv.*
suffer, **patior, pati, passus sum.**
sufficiently, sufficient, **satis,** *adv.*
suitable, **idoneus, a, um.**
suited, **accommodātus, a, um.**
Sulla, **Sulla, ae,** *m.*
summer, **aestas, ātis,** *f.*
summon, **voco, āre, āvi, ātum.**
supplies, **commeātus, us,** *m.,* *used in both sing. and plural.*
support, **sublĕvo, āre, āvi, ātum.**
suppose, **existĭmo, āre, āvi, ātum;** than we, you suppose, than any one supposes, *after a comparative, may be rendered by* **opiniōne;** *see* L<small>N</small> XXXIII., R<small>EF</small>. 1–3.

suppress, **comprĭmo, ĕre, pressi, pressum.**
surely, **profecto,** *adv.*
surpass, excel, **antecello, ĕre,** *no perf. nor sup.;* **supĕro. āre.**
surrender, **dedo, ĕre, dedĭdi, dedĭtum;** a surrender, **dedĭtio, ōnis,** *f.*
surround, **circumdo, āre, dĕdi, dătum.**
suspicion, **suspicio, ōnis,** *f.*
swamp, **palus, ūdis,** *f.*
Swiss, **Helvetii, ōrum,** *m. pl.*
Switzerland, **Helvetia, ae,** *f.*
sword, **gladius, i,** *m.*

T.

take, **capio, capĕre, cepi, captum;** take away, **removeo, ĕre, mōvi, mōtum;** take from, **eripio, eripĕre, eripui, ereptum;** take part, be engaged *in anything,* **versor, āri, ātus sum;** take place, **geror, i, gestus sum;** take possession of, **occŭpo, āre, āvi, ātum,** *w. acc.*
tax, **stipendium, i,** *n.*
teach, **doceo, ēre, docui, doctum.**
teacher, **praeceptor, ōris,** *m.*
tell, **dico, ĕre, dixi, dictum; narro, āre, āvi, ātum.**
temple, **templum, i,** *n.*
tenth, **decĭmus, a, um.**
terms, **condicio, ōnis,** *f.;* in very strong terms, **amplissĭmis verbis.**
terrify, **perterreo, ēre, ui, ĭtum.**

territory, **fines, ium,** *m. pl.*
than, **quam,** *adv.; see also* Ln. XXXIII., Ref. 1–3.
thank, **gratias ago, agĕre, egi, actum.**
thankful, feel thankful, **gratiam habeo, ēre, ui, ĭtum.**
thanksgiving, **supplicatio (subplicatio), ōnis,** *f.*
that, **ille, is,** *dem. pron's; see* Ln. IV., Ref. 1–8; that, in order that, **ut;** that not, **ne, ut non;** *see* Lessons VII.–X.
the ... the, **quanto ... tanto; quo ... eo;** *see* Ln. XXXIII., Ref. 7–9.
the one ... the other, **alter ... alter;** the one party ... the other, **altĕri ... altĕri.**
the other, **cetĕrus, a, um.**
the same, **idem;** at one and the same time, **simul,** *adv.;* at the same time, **eōdem tempŏre,** *or* **uno tempŏre;** the same ... as, **idem ... qui.**
the second time, **itĕrum,** *adv.*
their, **suus, a, um,** *when referring to same person or thing as the subject of its sentence, otherwise* **eōrum.**
there, in that place, **ibi,** *adv.*
think, **puto, āre, āvi, ātum; arbĭtror, āri, ātus sum;** think upon, think of, **cogĭto, āre, āvi, ātum;** *w. acc.*
this, **hic,** *see* Ln. IV., Ref. 1–8.
threaten, **immineo, ēre,** *no perf. nor sup.;* threaten frequently or much, **minĭtor, āri, ātus sum.**

threats, **minae, ārum,** *f. pl.*
through, throughout, **per,** *prep. w. acc.*
throw back, **rejicio, jicĕre, jēci, jectum**; throw into disorder, **perturbo, āre, āvi, ātum,**
thwart, **obsto, stāre, stĭti, stātum.**
till, cultivate, **colo, ĕre, colui, cultum.**
till, until, **dum, donec, quoad,** *conj's*; till late at night, **ad multam noctem.**
time, **tempus, ŏris,** *n.*; for all time, in perpetuum, *sc.* **tempus**; at one and the same time, **simul,** *adv.*; now for a long time, **jam diu, jam dudum,** *adv's*; the second time, a second time, **itĕrum,** *adv.*
to, **ad,** *prep. w. acc.*
to be feared, **pertimescendus, a, um.**
to-day, **hodie,** *adv.*; **hodiernus dies, hodierni diēi,** *m.*
together with, **una cum,** *w. abl.*
top of, **summus, a, um**
torch, **fax, facis,** *f.*
towards, **ad,** *prep. w. acc.*
tower, **turris, is,** *f., acc. sing.* **turrim.**
town, **oppĭdum, i,** *n.*
transport, **transporto, āre, āvi, ātum.**
treason, **proditio, ōnis,** *f.*
tribe, **natio, ōnis,** *f.*
tribune, **tribūnus, i,** *m.*
tributary, **vectigālis, e.**
tried, **probātus, a, um.**
triple, three-fold, **triplex,** *gen.* **triplĭcis.**

Trojan, **Trojānus, a, um.**
troops, **copiae, ārum,** *f. pl.*
trouble, **calamĭtas, ātis,** *f.*; **malum, i,** *n.*
troubled, anxious, **sollicĭtus (solicĭtus), a, um.**
true, **verus, a, um.**
trusting to, **fretus, a, um,** *w. abl.*
truth, **verum, i,** *n.*
try, **experior, īri, expertus sum.**
twice, **bis,** *num. adv.*
two, **duo, duae, duo.**

U.

unacquainted with, **ignārus, a, um,** *see* Ln. XXIII., Ref. 6-12.
under, **sub,** *prep. w. acc.*
understand, **intellĕgo, ĕre, lexi, lectum.**
unfortunate, **miser, misĕra, misĕrum.**
unfriendly, **inimīcus, a, um.**
unite, **conjungo, ĕre, junxi, junctum,** *w. pers. pron.*
unjustly, **injuria,** *abl. of manner.*
unless, **nisi,** *conj.*
unoccupied, be unoccupied, **vaco, āre, āvi, ātum.**
unpopularity, **invidia, ae,** *f.*
until, till, **dum, donec, quoad,** *conj's.*; *see* Ln. XV., Ref. 8-10.
unusual, **inusitātus, a, um.**
unwilling, **invītus, a, um**; be unwilling, **nolo, nolle, nolui**; I shall be unwilling to come, **invītus veniam.**
upon, **in,** *prep. w. acc.*
urge, **cohortor, āri, ātus sum.**
use, **utor, uti, usus sum.**

V.

valor, **virtus, ūtis,** *f.*
variety, **variĕtas, ātis,** *f.*
very, **valde,** *adv.;* see also LN. II., NOTE 3 ; *when a noun is to be emphasized,* **ipse** *is used:* e. g. the very city, **urbs ipsa.**
very difficult, **perdifficĭlis, e.**
very many, **permulti, ae, a.**
very much, **vehementer,** *adv.*
vicinity, in *or* into the vicinity of, **ad,** *prep. w. acc.*
vicissitude, **variĕtas, ātis,** *f.*
victory, **victoria, ae,** *f.*
vigorously, **acrĭter,** *adv.*
village, **vicus, i,** *m.*
villainy, **scelus, ĕris,** *n.*
violence, **vis, vis,** *f.*
violent hands, see lay.
visit, **viso, ĕre, visi, visum.**
voice, **vox, vocis,** *f.*

W.

wage, carry on, **gero, ĕre, gessi, gestum.**
wagon, **carrus, i,** *m.*
wait for, await, wait *to see,* **exspecto (expecto), āre, āvi, ātum.**
wait for **praestōlor, āri, ātus sum.**
wall, **murus, i,** *m. generic term;* **moenia, ium,** *n. pl.,* CITY WALLS, RAMPARTS, BULWARKS; **paries pariĕtis,** *m.,* WALL OF A HOUSE.
war, **bellum, i,** *n.*
watches, **vigiliae, ārum,** *f. pl.*
way, **via, ae,** *f.*

weapon, **telum, i,** *n.*
weep, **fleo, flere, flevi, fletum.**
weight, **pondus, ĕris,** *n.*
welfare, prosperity, **salus, ūtis,** *f.;* highest welfare of the government, **summum imperium.**
well, **bene,** *adv.*
what sort of a, **qui, quae, quod,** *interr. pron.*
wheel about, **signa converto, ĕre, verti, versum.**
when, **cum (quum), ubi,** *adv's.*
whence, **unde,** *adv.*
where, **ubi,** *adv.*
whether, **utrum, num, — ne,** see LN. XVI.
while, **dum,** *conj.;* for a little while, **paulisper,** *adv.;* it is worth while, **tanti est,** see LN. XXIII., REF. 1-5; a little while ago, **paulo ante.**
whither, **quo,** *adv.*
who, which, what, **qui, quae, quod,** *rel. pron.;* **quis, quae, quid,** *and* **qui, quae, quod,** *interrog. pron.;* who is to, who was to, ETC., see LN. VII., NOTE 1 ; who pray ? **quis tandem?**
whole, wholly, see all.
why, **cur, quid,** see LN. XXX., REF. 1-6.
wicked, **imprŏbus, a, um.**
wide, **latus, a, um.**
widely, **late,** *adv.*
wife, **uxor, ōris,** *f.;* **conjux, ŭgis,** *f.*
willing, be willing, **volo, velle, volui.**
win a victory, **victoriam vinco, ĕre, vici, victum.**

wing, **cornu, us,** *n.;* on the right wing, **a dextro cornu.**
winter, **hiems, hiĕmis,** *f.;* pass the winter, **hiĕmo, āre, āvi, ātum;** winter-quarters, **hiberna, ōrum,** *n. pl., sc.* **castra.**
wisdom, **sapientia, ae,** *f.*
wise, **sapiens,** *gen.* **sapientis.**
wish, desire, be willing, **volo, velle, volui.**
with, in company with, **cum,** *prep. w. abl.;* with, near to, at the house of, **apud,** *prep. w. acc.;* with respect to, **de,** *prep. w. abl.*
withdraw, **deficio, ficĕre, fēci, fectum;** to withdraw from allegiance to the king, **a rege deficĕre;** withdraw, betake one's self, **se recipio, cipĕre, cēpi, ceptum.**
without, **sine,** *prep. w. abl.;* be without, **careo, ēre, ui, ītum,** *w. abl.*
withstand, **obsto, stāre, stĭti, stātum,** *w. dat.;* **sustineo, ēre, ui, tentum,** *w. acc.;* to withstand an attack, **impĕtum sustinēre.**
witness, **testis,** *m. and f.*

worthy, **dignus, a, um;** it is worth while, **tanti est,** *see* LN. XXIII., REF. 1-5.
would that, *see* LN. V., REF. 8, 9.
wound, **vulnus, (volnus) ĕris,** *n.;* to wound, **vulnĕro, (volnĕro), āre, āvi, ātum.**
wretch, **scelerātus, i,** *m.*
write, **scribo, ĕre, scripsi, scriptum.**
wrong, **injuria, ae,** *f.*

Y.

year, **annus, i,** *m.*
yesterday, **hesterno die;** day before yesterday, **nudius tertius (nunc, dies, tertius).**
yet, **tamen,** *adv.*
young, **juvĕnis, e.**
your, **tuus, a, um,** *when addressing one person;* **vester, vestra, vestrum,** *when addressing more than one.*

Z.

zeal, **studium, i,** *n.*
zealous, **studiōsus, a, um.**

www.ingramcontent.com/pod-product-compliance
Lightning Source LLC
Chambersburg PA
CBHW030320170426
43202CB00009B/1086